just like me knits

brandy fortune

POTTER CRAFT
NEW YORK

For Sydney and Rowan, who always inspire me, and for Jesse, who always supports me.

Published in the United States by Potter Craft, an imprint of the Crown Publishing Group, a division of Random House, Inc., New York.
www.crownpublishing.com
wwww.pottercraft.com

POTTER CRAFT and colophon is a registered trademark of Random House, Inc.

Library of Congress Cataloging-in-Publication Data
Fortune, Brandy.
Just like me knits / Brandy Fortune. -- First Edition.
pages cm
Includes index.
1. Knitting--Patterns. 2. Children's clothing. I. Title.
TT825.F67 2013
746.43'2--dc23
2012020351

ISBN 978-0-307-58708-4
eISBN 978-0-7704-3437-3

Printed in China

Design by La Tricia Watford
Photography by Brandy Fortune
Illustrations on page 9 used with the permission of Rachelle Anne Miller

The author and publisher would like to thank the Craft Yarn Council of America for providing the yarn weight standards and accompanying icons used in this book. For more information, please visit www.YarnStandards.com.

10 9 8 7 6 5 4 3 2 1

First Edition

contents

Foreword

Quite a few years ago I started listening to knitting podcasts. There weren't many around at that time. It was the early days for the pairing of technology and knitting. One day I was checking to see if any new knitting podcasts had become available and I ran across the Pixie Purls podcast. The host was a bright, cheerful young woman from Georgia who earnestly explored knitting and shared her findings through her podcast and blog. I loved listening to who I now know is none other than Brandy Fortune.

I followed along to every episode and blog post, as Brandy became a mother for the first time and then the second time. She dove into parenthood headfirst and fell head over heels in love with all that it entails, similar to the way she embraces her knitting. I could relate to Brandy on so many levels. I started my own knitting career with little ones on my lap and running around at my feet. It is not an easy thing to do.

With dewy love and appreciation for parenthood, Brandy began designing knitwear for her young daughters. Through her firsthand experience with young children and years of knitting experience, Brandy knows exactly what knitters want in a pattern. Her designs always hit the mark for beautiful simplicity, practicality, and an uncanny understanding of what and how knitters want to knit, especially when it comes to knitting for children. This combination of experience, skill, and understanding is a rare find.

It was a few years ago that Brandy noticed an unfilled gap in the online knitting community and it was in line with her own interests in knitting as the mother of two young children. Brandy and Allegra Wermuth, her online knitting friend and fellow parent, began moving into uncharted territory by creating an online magazine, PetitePurls.com, that offers children's knitting patterns along with articles and features about parenthood and living a creative lifestyle. Petite Purls also put Brandy's other love (yes, there is another love), photography, at the forefront. Brandy photographs many of the knitwear designs and beauty shots for Petite Purls. With her bag overflowing with skills, Brandy is one of the most talented and versatile young knitting designers in the industry today. She does it all with great style, passion, and love.

Brandy's quick rise in the knitting industry does not surprise me. She has worked hard, and it is clear she has an undeniable passion for her work. When I heard she was writing a knitting book I immediately became excited. Of course, it would be a thoughtful, beautiful book of knits for young children. When I learned that Brandy was photographing and designing everything in the book, I knew with certainty that it would become a treasured and well-used collection for years to come. She has taken her experience as a parent, her nostalgia and current love of dolls and educational toys, and her passion for childhood and its adventures, and combined it all to create this book in front of you.

The only way to truly understand Brandy's passion for children, learning, and knitting is to dive right into the pages of this innovative book she has thoughtfully created. With nearly thirty-eight knitting patterns (nineteen patterns for children and matching patterns for dolls), hand-sewing basics, and five sewing patterns, this book is destined to become a great resource for generations to come.

Brandy is a role model for our online knitting community. She is deeply rooted in family, in living a creative lifestyle, in taking the time to nurture and appreciate children, and in making the world a better place. She is passionate and earnest to a fault and that is apparent in the pages ahead of you.

I encourage you to take Brandy's lead as an example of knitting for the small but always living large at the same time!

Susan B. Anderson

introduction

If you had told me seven years ago that not only would I be a knitter, but that I would be a knitwear designer and author, I would not have believed you. But when my husband and I settled down in a small suburb of Atlanta, we purchased an acre of land for our dogs and, with plans to have kids, I suddenly felt very lost and out of touch. I was bored in our quiet house and signed up for what I thought was a crochet class at a local yarn shop. In that first class I was informed we would most certainly not be learning how to crochet and that I must go buy some needles. *Why not*, I thought, *this could be fun*. So began my knitting adventures. A few years later my first daughter, Sydney, was born, and suddenly I found myself at a loss for knitting patterns that I actually wanted—and had time—to knit. When Sydney was six months of age, I designed my first children's pattern, just for her.

And now, five years later, this book began just as simply, with a sweet little hooded jacket I worked up in garter stitch for one of my daughter's dolls (Katie Garter Jacket, page 14). I'd recently become a bit obsessed with the Waldorf-style cloth dolls made of natural materials and found myself doing some online stalking to see if I could get a handcrafted Bamboletta Doll—for my daughters, of course, although the truth is that I may love them even more than they do.

The idea of a doll, made by hand and of natural materials, made sense to me as a parent and double sense to me as a knitter who could appreciate the handspun and dyed yarn hair, as well as the hand-carded wool stuffed inside. Today's doll makers add funky colors and textures to the hair, a splash of color to the eyes and a smile, a bit of rose to the cheeks and tiny freckles on the nose. They are just too adorable to resist. When a mom is stuck in a chair with a baby asleep on her lap and a computer within typing distance, she's bound to be up to no good! In my case a few of these dolls quickly became a collection. I have no doubt that eighty-plus years ago there was a mother in a rocking chair ogling the Sears, Roebuck and Company catalog. Husbands like mine may not approve of this sort of activity, but my mom always said that if the mother is happy, the baby is happy!

So there I sat with several handmade dolls, one of which I was able to customize to look like Sydney. I gave it to her as a special present on the day we brought her little sister, Rowan, home from the hospital. To draw my eldest daughter into playtime, I began designing clothes for her doll with special kid-size outfits to match. Sydney loves when things match, but it was always difficult to find doll clothes, even for commercially available dolls, that matched her wardrobe. The clothing choices were either too limited or costly. I can't tell you how many times I thought to myself *I just want to put my girls in tops and jeans, and have their dolls match!*

With *Just Like Me Knits*, your child can dress his or her favorite doll in the clothes he or she likes best. In these pages you will find nineteen projects for boys and girls in a range of sizes, from 12 months to 12 years, with matching projects to knit for their favorite dolls and stuffed toys. You can knit everyday favorites such as a striped raglan sweater, perfect for an adventurous boy to run around in (Aiden Pullover, page 29); fancy dress-up clothes such as a fun and sparkly skirt (Kaylee Beaded Skirt, page 75); and accessories for mother, child, and doll, such as beautiful and intricate knee-high lace socks (Samantha Lace Kneesocks, page 114).

As the mother of two young, energetic children I must admit to you that I am a pragmatic knitter. This does not mean I don't challenge myself with complex stitches or patterns, but it does mean that when I knit I like to keep things simple—and fast. My goal with these patterns is to create unique and well-executed garments with the least amount of work. I like a quick, clean knit that is accessible to new knitters, yet interesting for those with advanced skills. You'll find sizing, measuring, and customization help in Before You Begin (page 8) and a quick primer to techniques and resources at the back of the book. I've also included a short guide to hand-sewing basic doll clothes, with five original patterns to create complete outfits for any doll or toy.

Making clothes for my children allows me to be creative and to connect with them while still entertaining myself. It is one of those wonderful distractions a young mother likes to have to keep her mind off the dirty diapers and dishes.

BEFORE YOU BEGIN

When designing patterns, I try to fill the gaps in available patterns and what I want to knit for my own children and nephews: more designs for boys, kids, and tweens. That's why in this book, I use size conventions from 12 months to 12 years, but as many parents have experienced, there's a lot of wiggle room with children's sizing. My toddler's jeans suddenly become capris when my four-year-old tries them on—and my nephew was wearing size 24-month T-shirts when he was about a year old. When knitting for a little person, it's always best to compare the child's measurements with the finished measurements given for the pattern. If you are unsure which size to choose, it's always best to knit "up" a size so that the child can grow into your hand-knit gift. I've also included some customization tips below for easy pattern size adaptations and yarn substitutions.

The doll patterns in this book are designed for 15-inch-tall (38cm) cloth-bodied dolls, but most also will fit nicely on plastic 18-inch (45.5cm) dolls, as well as small stuffed toys. Similar to the child-size patterns, doll clothing can be adjusted easily to accommodate dolls that are taller, shorter, thicker, longer-limbed, or with heads of different sizes. Taking a few quick measurements of your child and their favorite doll or toy will prepare you to make any adjustments necessary to ensure a good fit.

Customizing Patterns

Altering sizing for children and dolls is much simpler than it would be for an adult, which would have hip and bust shaping to get in the way of the easy math. One trick that works well on small patterns, such as doll and infant sweaters, is the simplest: *Go up a needle size.* This will increase the stitch gauge and row height and can be the perfect solution to making something fit much better without doing any math!

For specific alterations, use the following tips to knit for a perfect fit. The same guidelines apply when hand-sewing doll clothes (Just Like Me Sewing, page 140).

sleeve length

Adjusting sleeve length just might be the easiest change to make. Simply increase or decrease the number of rows knit close to the top of the sleeve—after any sleeve increases when working from the bottom up, or after separating the sleeve from the body when working top-down designs. Be sure to note the numbers of rows you knit for each sleeve so that they are of equal length.

skirt, pants, and dress lengths

It's best to increase or decrease rows in areas without shaping. For skirts, that usually means after hip increases and before any edging, and for pants, the safest place is above the knee, to avoid interrupting any hip or lower leg shaping. For a dress the bottom can easily be increased a few inches before the border to add height.

body length

If the body of a simple garment, such as a sweater, is knit top-down, then you will adjust the pattern below the underarm shaping. For example, a pattern may instruct you to "continue in pattern as established until it measures 3 inches (7.5cm) from underarm," or similar. This is the section in which you will add extra length or remove it if needed.

If a garment is knit from the bottom up, or in pieces, you will add or remove length after the bottom border and before the armhole shaping.

MAKING MEASUREMENTS

I use the following measurements as a reference when designing for babies and children

	INFANT & TODDLER					CHILDREN			
size (in inches)	**6 mo**	**12 mo**	**18 mo**	**24mo**	**4 yrs**	**6 yrs**	**8 yrs**	**10yrs**	**12 yrs**
actual chest circumference	19"	20"	20½"	21"	22"	23½"	25"	27"	29"
garment length to underarm	7"	7½"	8"	8½"	9½"	10½"	11½"	12"	12½"
neck circumference	3½"	3½"	3½"	4"	4"	4"	4½"	4½"	5"
sleeve length (cuff to arm)	6"	7"	8"	9"	11¾"	13"	14¼"	15½"	15½"

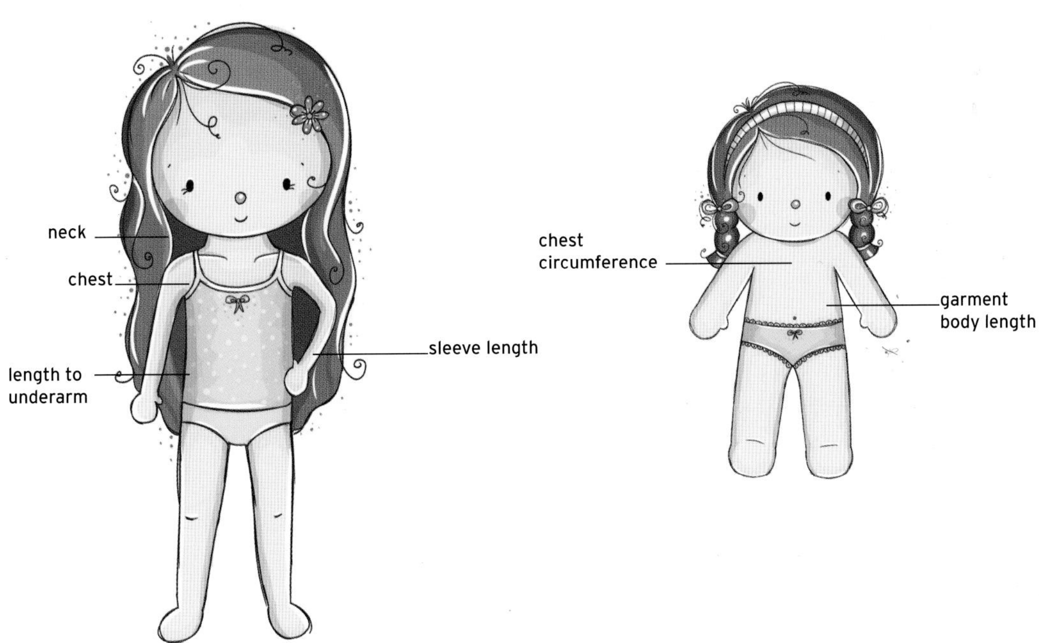

When adjusting length, you must note any design elements in the body, such as allover stitch patterns, and use your best judgment in adding or subtracting pattern rows or additional design repeats. Start by having a clear idea of what you want the pattern to look like, and plan ahead.

body width from the bottom up

Making a pattern larger or smaller around the chest and torso is simplest when knitting a pattern from the bottom up, such as the Brett Deer Vest (page 21). Just cast on more, or fewer, stitches and improvise as you go. When resizing a garment with a repeating stitch pattern, ensure that your new cast-on number reflects that stitch count repeat. For example, to make sure that a lace pattern with a 7-stitch repeat (as in the Sydney Lace Dress, page 62) works out properly, you must either add or subtract 7 to or from the cast-on.

Keep in mind that a few stitches can make a big change to a tiny doll-sized garment and use your gauge (stitches per inch [cm]) as a guide. If you do make a mistake, chances are that such a small piece of clothing will still fit, and no one will be the wiser.

body width from the top down

When customizing a pattern worked from the top down, you will need to be a bit clever in how you change your stitch count. If you look at any of the children's patterns, you will see differences in the number of stitches worked for each size. For example, the cast-on number changes, and the number of increase or decrease rounds may change. Making these types of overall sizing changes for yourself is one of those things that seem far more intimidating than they actually are. Let's use the Aiden Doll Pullover (page 33) as an example.

Adjust the cast-on: Say you had knit this pullover and found the overall pattern to be about 1 inch (2.5cm) too wide. Your gauge is set at 5 stitches per inch, so you know you need to remove 5 stitches overall. The pattern reads as follows:

> With MC, cast on 38 stitches, placing markers as follows: 8 (right back), 2 (sleeve), 18 (front), 2 (sleeve), 8 (left back).

There are only 2 sleeve stitches for each sleeve, so we don't want to remove any of those—and they would not affect the width of the torso even if we did. Instead, we are going to remove an even number of stitches from the front and back. To make the adjustment easier, let's round down from 5 stitches to 4. Our new pattern will read:a

> With MC, cast on 34 stitches, placing markers as follows: 7 (right back), 2 (sleeve), 16 (front), 2 (sleeve), 7 (left back).

We have removed 2 stitches from the front (18 is now 16) and 1 stitch from each side of the back (each 8 becomes a 7). This tiny adjustment doesn't seem like much, but on doll clothing 1 inch (2.5cm) can make a large difference. It is easy to see how you can apply this same technique to subtract or add 2 or 3 inches (5 or 7.5cm): Just remove or add more stitches, using your gauge as a guide.

Adjust the armhole depth and sleeve width: Now look closely at the armhole increases. The pattern continues, and the 12 raglan sleeve increases read as follows:

> **Next row (increase):** With CC *knit to 1 stitch before the marker, kfb, slip the marker, kfb; repeat from * 3 times more, knit to the end.

Next row: Purl.

Repeat last two rows 11 times more, making sure to continue in the Stripe pattern.

This pattern has 12 sleeve increases made over 24 rows. If you need the sleeves to be smaller and the armholes to be shorter, try 9 or 10 repeats total instead of 12. Now try the pullover on the doll to determine whether you need to work any additional repeats for a proper fit. Huzzah! You have just changed the design all by yourself.

Use this strategy to upsize and downsize both child- and doll-size patterns. If this is your first attempt at customization, tackle the easier patterns first and then move on to the more advanced projects.

Substituting Yarn

When choosing yarns for the projects in this book, I focused on fiber—from wearable, washable cotton and cotton blends to lightweight wools that won't stretch out when knit. I've factored things like durability and stretch into the patterns, so if substituting yarn, it's important to choose a fiber as close to the listed yarn as possible. And always make sure your gauge matches the gauge listed for the pattern, regardless of the fiber content.

A NEW GENERATION OF DOLLS

Each generation of children has a particular style of doll they remember for the rest of their lives. Cabbage Patch Kids, Cricket, Barbie, and Strawberry Shortcake dolls are just a few that I recall from my childhood. Today, our children have so many options, from dolls popular worldwide to handmade friends found online and at craft fairs. With this in mind, I designed the patterns in this book to fit most any doll you can find. Use the tips in this section to make simple adjustments, such as lengthening sleeves or widening the body. Dive right in, knit an outfit, and a child will soon find a doll to dress up.

CHAPTER ONE everyday

One thing my toddler likes to do more than anything is to help. "Hew Daddy! Hew Mommy!" she says with such happiness as she hands me a bit of trash or a bottle cap. She wants to help wash, she wants to help pour. Such everyday chores are made magnificent through her eyes. For me, the everyday designs you'll find in the pages that follow are anything but ordinary—a dainty pinafore for watering tomatoes in the garden (Reagan Pinafore, page 53), a woodland vest for tree climbing and treasure hunting (Brett Deer Vest, page 21).

One helpful activity is playing wash day. All kids need is a bucket filled with bubbles (and maybe a bit of real soap so they actually do some cleaning) and a small clothesline set up within reach. I found my galvanized bucket at the hardware store and a little washboard at an antique shop. My girls love to bring their doll clothing outside and start "scrubbing." I'm always surprised at how busy this keeps them, how clean they get the clothes, and how much I enjoy the time outside, too.

katie garter jacket

Knit in a chunky gauge, this simple cotton jacket looks lovely worn over a spring dress with a bold pattern. Wooden toggles complement the style and add the perfect finishing touch. I designed it in a multitude of smaller sizes as the heavy yarn works best on a smaller scale. This pattern is such a fast knit that you may want to make one every year.

skill level

Easy

sizes

1 (2, 3, 4, 5, 6) years.
Shown in size 2 years.

finished measurements

Chest circumference: 26 (27, 27¾, 28, 28¾, 29)" (66 [68.5, 70.5, 71, 73, 74] cm)

Length: 11 (12¾, 13½, 14¼, 15, 16)" (28 [32.5, 34.5, 36, 38, 40.5]cm)

materials

- Blue Sky Alpacas Worsted Multi Cotton, 100% cotton; 2⅜ oz (67g), 100 yd (91m); 4 (5, 6, 6, 6, 7) skeins in #6806 Icing (4)
- Size U.S. 7 (4.5mm) circular needle, 24" (61cm) length
- Size U.S. 7 (4.5mm) double-pointed needles for sleeves, or size to obtain gauge
- Size U.S. G (4mm) or H (5mm) crochet hook
- 4 stitch markers
- 6 safety pins
- 2 stitch holders
- Darning needle
- 3 wooden toggles, 1¼" long
- Sewing needle and thread

gauge

4 stitches and 8 rows = 1" (2.5cm) in garter stitch

notes

Cast on the Hood with approximately 18" of excess yarn so that you can use it to seam up the top of the Hood when finished. If you prefer to pick up live stitches rather than seam, use your favorite cast-on for grafting stitches.

Refer to Special Stitches and Techniques (page 151) for instructions on the backward-loop cast-on and crochet slip stitch.

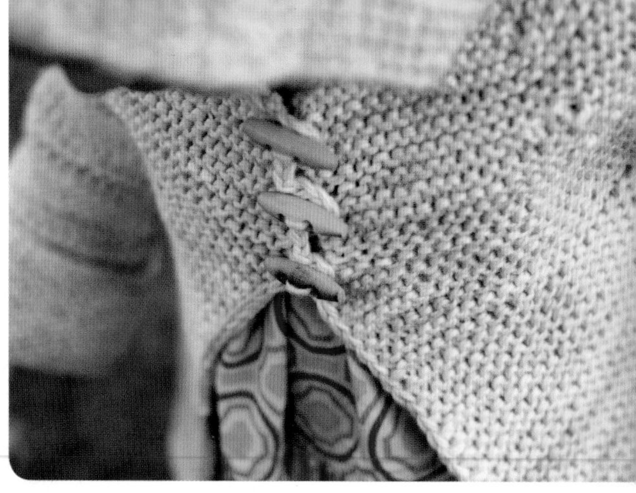

HOOD AND YOKE

Cast on 52 (64, 66, 68, 70, 72) stitches. *Make sure to cast on with a good bit of excess yarn that you can use to seam up the top of the hood later.* Work in garter stitch (knit every row) until piece measures 9¾ (10, 10¼, 10½, 10¾, 11)" (25 [25.5, 26, 26.5, 27.5, 28]cm) from the cast-on edge, ending on a right-side row.

Sizes 1 and 2 Only

Decrease row (WS): *K2tog; repeat from * to end—26 (32) stitches remain.

Sizes 3, 4, 5, and 6 Only

Decrease row (WS): K2 (3, 4, 5), [k2tog] 7 times, k2 (3, 4, 5), k2tog [15, 14, 13, 12] times, k2 (3, 4, 5), [k2tog] 7 times, k2 (3, 4, 5)—37 (40, 43, 46) stitches remain.

raglan shaping

Note: Mark the right side of the work with a safety pin so you will always know on which side to make the raglan increases.

Setup row (RS): Knit into the front and back of the stitch (kfb), place a marker, kfb, k3 (5, 7, 8, 9, 10), kfb, place a marker, kfb, k12 (14, 15, 16, 17, 18), kfb, place a marker, kfb, k3 (5, 7, 8, 9, 10), kfb, place a marker, kfb (8 stitches increased)—34 (40, 45, 48, 51, 54) stitches.

Next row: Knit.

Raglan Increase row: *Knit to 1 stitch before the marker, kfb, slip the marker, kfb; repeat from * 3 times more, knit to the end—42 (48, 53, 56, 59, 62) stitches.

Repeat last two rows twice. There are 5 stitches before the first marker and 5 stitches after the last marker—58 (64, 69, 72, 75, 78) stitches.

Next row: Knit.

Increase row: Kfb, *knit to 1 stitch before the marker, kfb, slip the marker, kfb; repeat from * 3 times more, knit to the last stitch, kfb (10 stitches increased)—68 (74, 79, 82, 85, 88) stitches.

Repeat last two rows twice. There are 11 stitches before the first marker and 11 stitches after the last marker—88 (94, 99, 102, 105, 108) stitches.

Next row: Knit to the end, then cast on 3 (4, 5, 5, 6, 6) stitches using the backward-loop cast-on.

Next row: *Knit to 1 stitch before the marker, kfb, slip the marker, kfb; repeat from * 3 times more, knit to the end, then cast on 3 (4, 5, 5, 6, 6) stitches—102 (110, 117, 120, 125, 128) stitches.

Continue to work in garter stitch, repeating the Raglan Increase row every 8 rows 3 times more (11 total increase rows)—126 (134, 141, 144, 149, 152) stitches.

Work even until raglan shaping measures 5 (5¾, 6, 6¼, 6½, 7)" (12.5 [14.5, 15, 15.5, 16.5, 18]cm) from shoulder, ending with a wrong-side row.

separate sleeves from body

Note: Increase stitches by using the backward-loop cast-on.

Next row (RS): K19 (20, 21, 21, 22, 22) stitches for right front; cast on 4 stitches, place a marker, cast on 4 stitches; place the next 25 (27, 29, 30, 31, 32) sleeve stitches onto a holder; k38 (40, 41, 42, 43, 44) stitches for back; cast on 4 stitches, place a marker, cast on 4 stitches; place the next 25 (27, 29, 30, 31, 32) sleeve stitches onto a holder; k19 (20, 21, 21, 22, 22) stitches for left front—92 (96, 99, 100, 103, 104) stitches.

BODY

Work even in garter stitch for 1½" (3.8cm).

Increase row (RS): *Knit to 1 stitch before the marker, kfb, slip the marker, kfb; repeat from * once more, knit to the end—96 (100, 103, 104, 107, 108) stitches.

Continue in garter stitch, working an Increase row every 1½" (3.8cm) twice more—104 (108, 111, 112, 115, 116) stitches.

Work even in garter stitch until Body measures 6 (7, 7½, 8, 8½, 9)" (15 [18, 19, 20.5, 21.5, 23] cm) from underarm.

Bind off loosely.

SLEEVES (*make 2*)

Place sleeve stitches onto needle.

Setup row (WS): Using the backward-loop cast-on, cast on 4 stitches, k25 (27, 29, 30, 31, 32) sleeve stitches, cast on 4 stitches—33 (35, 37, 38, 39, 40) stitches.

Work back and forth in garter stitch until sleeve measures 8¾ (10¾, 11½, 12¼, 13, 13½)" (22.5 [27.5, 29.5, 31, 33, 34.5]cm) for fold-back cuffs, as shown in the sample, or 6¼ (8¼, 9, 9¾, 10½, 11)" (15.5 [21, 23, 25, 26.5, 28]cm) for straight sleeves.

Bind off loosely.

Repeat for second sleeve.

FINISHING

Mark the 3 toggle or button placements on the left front, using safety pins, and then mark the corresponding garter ridge on the right front for the buttonhole loop placement.

CROCHET SLIP STITCH EDGING

Begin the slip stitch edging at the lower right front corner of the jacket, using the crochet hook. When you come to your desired toggle marker, *chain 4 stitches, skip the marked ridge and slip stitch to the next marker; repeat from * for the next two markers, then continue around the entire edge of the jacket including the bottom edge and hood. When you come back around to where you started you may want to slip an extra stitch back into the first crochet slip stitch to close the edging. Attach toggles; sew sleeve seams. Weave in long ends, as cotton can slip out a bit from wear and washing.

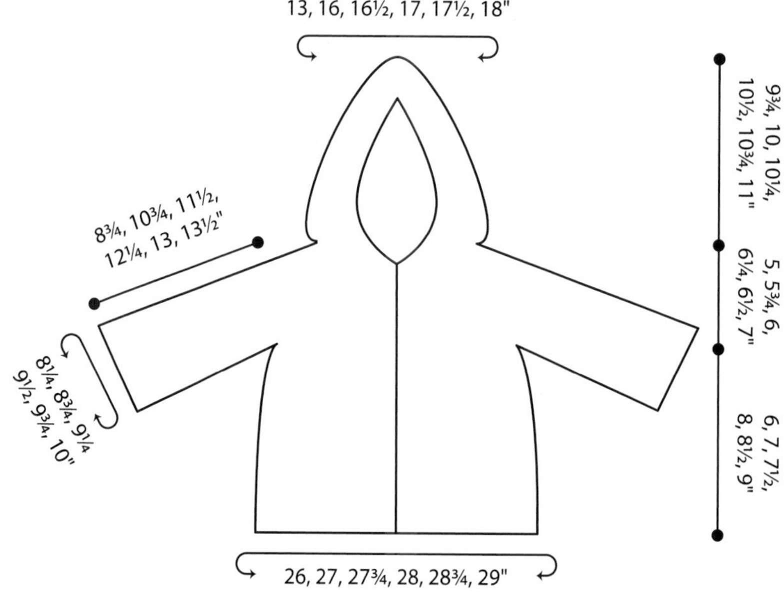

katie doll garter jacket

skill level

Easy

finished measurement

Chest circumference: 11–13" (28–33cm)

materials

- Blue Sky Alpacas Worsted Multi Cotton, 100% cotton; 2 3⁄8 oz (67g), 100 yd (91m); 2 skeins in #6804 Limeade (4)
- Size U.S. 7 (4.5mm) circular needle, 24" (61cm) length, or size needed to obtain gauge
- 4 stitch markers
- 2 stitch holders
- Safety pin
- Darning needle
- 1 button, 1⁄2" (13mm)

gauge

4 stitches and 8 rows = 1" (2.5cm) in garter stitch

notes

Cast on the hood with approximately 18" of excess yarn so that you can use it to seam up the top of the hood when finished. If you prefer to pick up live stitches, rather than seam, use your favorite cast-on for grafting stitches. Refer to Special Stitches and Techniques (page 151) for instructions on the backward-loop cast-on and crochet slip stitch.

HOOD AND YOKE

Cast on 46 stitches and work in garter stitch (knit every row) until piece measures 6½" (16.5cm), ending with a wrong-side row.

Decrease row (RS): K1, *k2tog, k2; repeat from * to last stitch, k1–35 stitches remain.

raglan increases

Note: Mark the right side of the work with a safety pin so you will always know on which side to make the raglan increases.

Next row (WS): K6, place a marker, k7, place a marker, k9, place a marker, k7, place a marker, k6.

Row 1 (RS): Knit into the front and back of the stitch (kfb), *knit to 1 stitch before the marker, kfb, slip the marker, kfb; repeat from * 3 times more, knit to the last stitch, kfb.

Row 2: Knit.

Repeat rows 1 and 2 once more.

Buttonhole row (RS): K2, yarn over, k2tog, *knit to 1 stitch before the marker, kfb, slip the marker, kfb; repeat from * 3 times more, knit to the end.

Next row: Knit.

Raglan Increase row (RS): *Knit to 1 stitch before the marker, kfb, slip the marker, kfb; repeat from * 3 times more, knit to the end.

Next row: Knit.

Repeat the last two rows 3 times more–95 stitches.

separate sleeves from body

Note: Increase stitches by using the backward-loop cast-on.

Next row (RS): K15 front stitches, place the next 21 sleeve stitches onto a holder, cast on 4 stitches, k23 back stitches, place the next 21 sleeve stitches onto a holder, cast on 4 stitches, k15 front stitches–61 stitches.

BODY

Work even in garter stitch for 3¼" (8cm). Bind off.

SLEEVES *(make 2)*

Place sleeve stitches onto needle.

Setup row (WS): Using the backward-loop cast-on, cast on 2 stitches, k21 sleeve stitches, cast on 2 stitches–25 stitches.

Work back and forth in garter stitch for 2½" (6.5cm).

Bind off.

Repeat for second sleeve.

FINISHING

Mark the button placement on the left front, using safety pins, and then mark the corresponding garter ridge on the right front for the buttonhole loop placement.

Sew sleeve seams and top of hood using the darning needle. Weave in the ends. Attach the button.

brett deer vest

For the adventurous boy or girl in your life, a whimsical silhouette of a stag emblazons the front of this woodland-themed vest. I knit this pattern in a lovely cotton-and-wool-blend yarn available in a breadth of fun colors, sure to please outdoor-loving kids of any age.

materials

- Spud & Chloë Sweater, 55% superwash wool, 45% organic cotton; 3½ oz (100g), 160 yd (146m); 2 (2, 3, 3, 3) skeins in #7515 Cider (4)
- Size U.S. 7 (4.5mm) circular needle, 16" (40.5cm) length, or size to obtain gauge
- Size U.S. 6 (4mm) circular needle, 16" (40.5cm) length
- Size U.S. 6 (4mm) double-pointed needles for sleeves
- 4 stitch markers
- 3 stitch holders
- Darning needle

gauge

4½ stitches and 6¼ rows = 1" (2.5cm) in stockinette stitch

notes

Refer to Special Stitches and Techniques (page 151) for instructions on the k1, p1 rib, three-needle bind-off, and grafting.

skill level
Intermediate

sizes
4 (6, 8, 10, 12) years.
Shown in size 8.

finished measurements
Chest circumference: 26 (27¾, 29¾, 31½, 33½)" (66 [70.5, 76, 82.5, 85.5]cm)
Length: 14 (15, 17, 18, 18¾)" (35.5 [38, 43, 45.5, 47.5] cm)

BODY

With smaller needle, cast on 100 (106, 112, 120, 128) stitches. Place a marker and join for working in the round.

Work in k1, p1 rib for 1½ inches (3.8cm).

Next round: Continue working the k1, p1 rib; place a second marker after 50 (53, 56, 60, 64) stitches to indicate side seam; continue established pattern to the end.

Change to the larger needle.

Body Increase round: *K9 (7, 7, 7, 8), knit through the front and back of the next stitch (kfb); repeat from * 9 (11, 13, 13, 13) times more, k0 (10, 0, 8, 2)–110 (118, 126, 134, 142) stitches.

Work even in stockinette stitch until body measures 2¼ (3, 4¼, 4½, 4¾)" (5.5 [7.5, 11, 11.5, 12]cm) from the cast-on edge.

Next round: K14 (16, 18, 20, 22), place a marker, work 27 stitches of Deer Chart, place a marker, k14 (16, 18, 20, 22), slip the marker, knit to end.

Continue as established, working Deer Chart on the front between the markers, and *at the same time*, when piece measures 8 (9, 10, 10½, 11)" (20.5 [23, 25.5, 26.5, 28]cm) from the cast-on edge, **divide for front and back** as follows:

Bind off 4 stitches, work in pattern as established to the side seam marker. Place the back stitches onto a holder to be worked later.

The remainder of the front will now be worked back and forth, reading chart from left to right on wrong-side rows.

FRONT

Next row (WS): Bind off 4 stitches, purl to the marker, work 27 stitches of Deer Chart, purl to the end–47 (51, 55, 59, 63) stitches remain.

Decrease row: K1, ssk, work in pattern as established to the last 3 stitches, k2tog, k1–45 (49, 53, 57, 61) stitches remain.

Repeat Decrease row every right-side row 0 (1, 2, 3, 4) times more–45 (47, 49, 51, 53) stitches remain.

Continue in pattern as established, working in stockinette stitch after completion of the chart, until piece measures 11 (12, 14, 15, 15¾)" (28 [30.5, 35.5, 38, 40]cm) from the cast-on edge, ending with a wrong-side row.

begin neck shaping

Next row: K18 (19 19, 20, 21), bind off the next 9 (9, 11, 11, 11) stitches, knit to the end.

right front

Row 1 (WS): Purl.

Rows 2 and 4: Bind off 2 stitches, knit to the end–14 (15, 15, 16, 17) stitches remain after row 4.

Row 3 and all wrong-side rows: Purl.

Rows 6, 8, 10, and 12: K1, ssk, knit to the end–10 (11, 11, 12, 13) stitches remain after row 12.

Continue in stockinette stitch until piece measures 14 (15, 17, 18, 18¾)" (35.5 [38, 43, 45.5, 47.5]cm) from the cast-on edge, ending with a wrong-side row.

Place stitches onto a holder.

left front

Join a new ball of yarn.

Rows 1 and 3 (WS): Bind off 2 stitches, purl to the end–14 (15, 15, 16, 17) stitches remain after row 3.

Rows 2 and 4: Knit.

Rows 5, 7, 9, and 11: Purl.

Rows 6, 8, 10, and 12: Knit to last 3 stitches, k2tog, k1–10 (11, 11, 12, 13) stitches remain after row 12.

Continue in stockinette stitch until piece measures 14 (15, 17, 18, 18¾)" (35.5 [38, 43, 45.5, 47.5]cm) from the cast-on edge, ending with a wrong-side row.

Place stitches onto a holder.

BACK

Place back stitches onto needle ready to work a right-side row. Working in stockinette stitch, bind off 4 stitches at the beginning of the next 2 rows–47 (51, 55, 59, 63) stitches remain.

Decrease row (RS): K1, ssk, knit to the last 3 stitches, k2tog, k1–45 (49, 53, 57, 61) stitches remain.

Repeat decrease row every right-side row 0 (1, 2, 3, 4) times more–45 (47, 49, 51, 53) stitches remain.

Work even in stockinette stitch until back measures 14 (15, 17, 18, 18¾)" (35.5 [38, 43, 45.5, 47.5]cm) from the cast-on edge, ending with a wrong-side row.

Next row: K10 (11, 11, 12, 13), bind off the next 25 (25, 27, 27, 27) stitches, knit to the end.

Place the front shoulder stitches onto needles. Join front and back shoulders using the three-needle bind-off, or graft stitches together.

ARMBANDS (*make 2*)

With the right side facing and smaller needle, starting at the center of the underarm, pick up and knit 56 (60, 66, 70, 72) stitches evenly around the armhole.

Work 5 rounds in k1, p1 rib.

Bind off in pattern.

NECK BAND

With the right side facing and smaller needle, starting at the right shoulder seam, pick up and knit 70 (70, 74, 74, 74) stitches evenly around the neck opening.

Work 5 rounds in k1, p1 rib.

Bind off in pattern.

FINISHING

Weave in the ends.

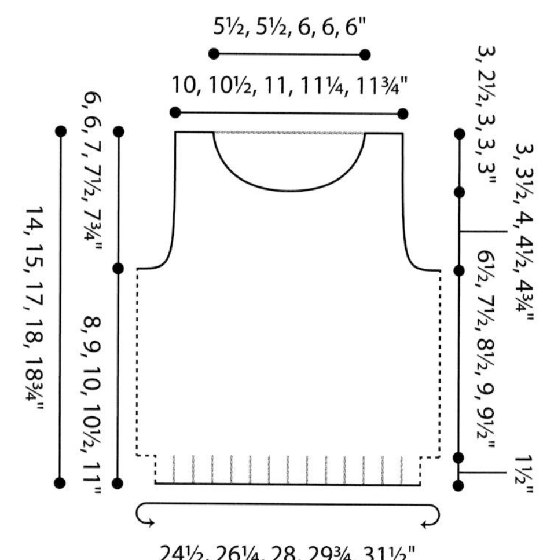

Deer Chart

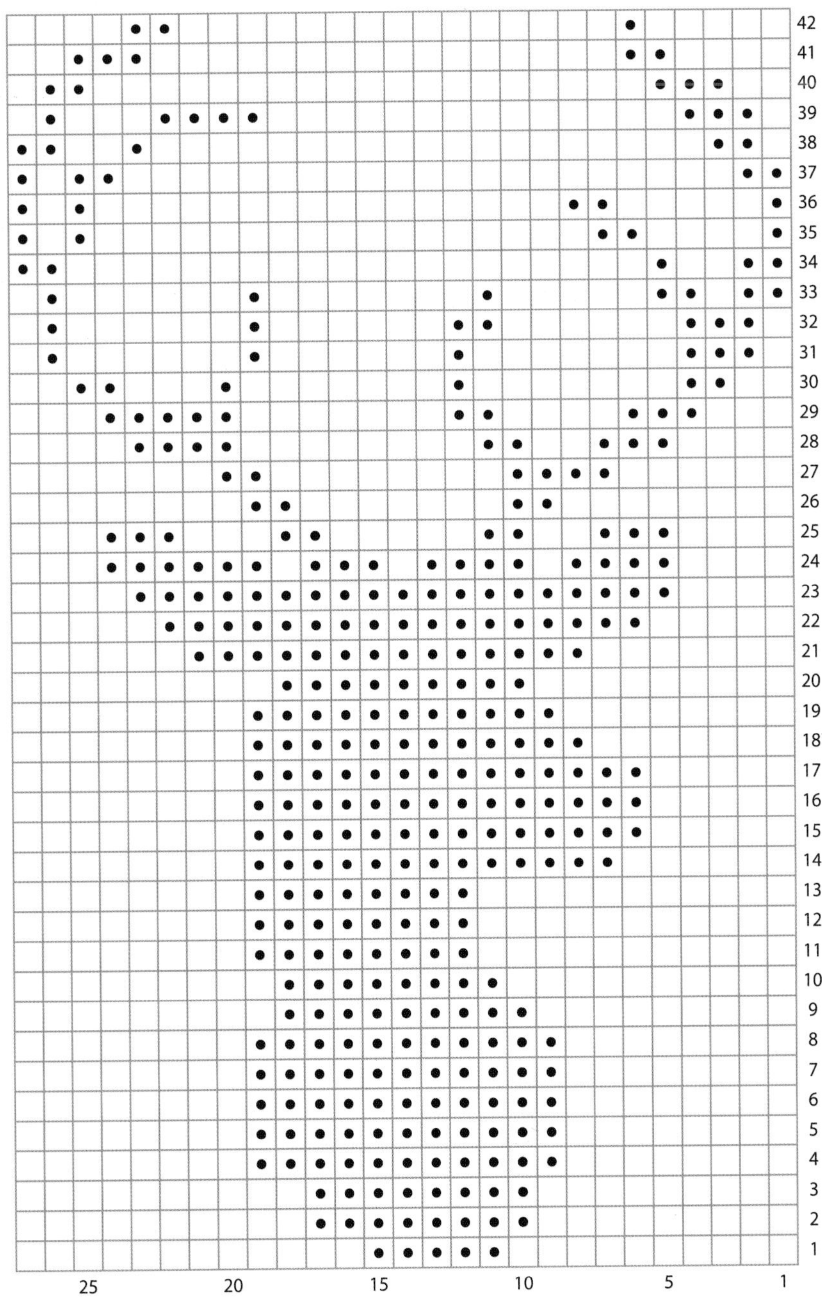

42
41
40
39
38
37
36
35
34
33
32
31
30
29
28
27
26
25
24
23
22
21
20
19
18
17
16
15
14
13
12
11
10
9
8
7
6
5
4
3
2
1
25
20
15
10
5
1
Key
knit
purl

brett doll deer vest

skill level
Intermediate

finished measurement
Chest circumference:
11–13" (28–33cm)

materials

- Spud & Chloë Sweater, 55% superwash wool, 45% organic cotton, 3½ oz (100g), 160 yd (146m), 1 skein in #7515 Cider (4)
- Size U.S. 7 (4.5mm) double-pointed needles, or circular needle for Magic Loop method
- Size U.S. 6 (4mm) double-pointed needles, or circular needle for Magic Loop method, or size to obtain gauge
- 2 stitch markers
- 2 buttons, ½" (13mm)
- Darning needle

gauge

4½ stitches and 6¼ rows = 1" (2.5cm) in stockinette stitch

notes

Refer to Special Stitches and Techniques (page 151) for instructions on the k1, p1 rib and Magic Loop method.

BODY

With smaller needle, cast on 62 stitches. Place a marker and join for working in the round.

Work 3 rounds in k1, p1 rib.

Change to larger needle. Work in stockinette stitch until sweater measures 3½" (9cm) from the cast-on edge.

Dividing round: K21 front stitches, bind off the next 10 stitches, k9, bind off the next 3 stitches, k9, bind off the next 10 stitches.

FRONT

Work in stockinette stitch over the next 21 stitches for 1½" (3.8cm).

Next row (RS): K5, bind off next 11 stitches, knit to the end.

left front

Continue in stockinette stitch on last 5 stitches for 1¾" (4.5cm). Bind off loosely.

right front

Attach yarn and work same as for left front.

LEFT BACK

With the WS facing, place 9 stitches on needles. Work in stockinette stitch for 3¼" (8cm). Bind off loosely.

RIGHT BACK

Attach yarn and work same as the left back.

SHOULDER SEAMS

Starting from the armhole edge, sew the 5 stitches of the left front to 5 stitches of the back, leaving the remaining 4 back stitches alone to later be picked up for neck band. Repeat for the right front.

ARMBANDS (*make 2*)

With the right side facing and smaller needle, starting at the center of the underarm, pick up and knit 32 stitches evenly around the armhole.

Work 3 rounds in k1, p1 rib.

Bind off in pattern.

NECK BAND

With the right side facing and smaller needle, starting at the left back center, pick up and knit 34 stitches evenly around neck opening, ending at the right back center.

Work 3 rows in k1, p1 rib.

Bind off in pattern.

RIGHT BACK PLACKET

With the right side facing and smaller needle, starting at the lower left edge of the back opening, pick up and knit 18 stitches evenly along the back opening and extra neck band.

Work 3 rounds in k1, p1 ribbing.

Bind off in pattern.

LEFT BACK PLACKET

With the right side facing and smaller needle, starting at the upper right edge of the neck band, pick up and knit 18 stitches evenly along the neck band and back opening.

Row 1 (WS): *K1, p1; repeat from * to end.

Row 2: [K1, p1] 3 times, k1, yarn over, k2tog, [p1, k1] twice, yarn over, k2tog, p1, k1, p1.

Row 3: Repeat row 1.

Bind off in pattern.

FINISHING

Place the left back placket over the right back placket and sew the bottom edges to the lower edge of the center back opening.

Attach buttons to the right back placket.

Weave in the ends.

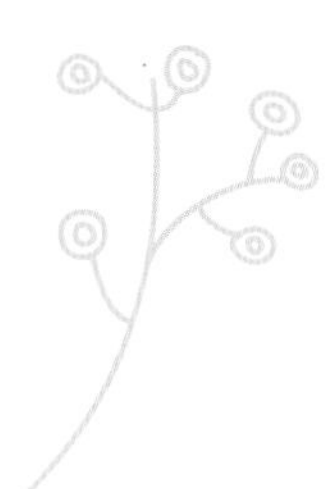

aiden pullover

When designing this sweater I imagined it to be a cross between a thermal ski top and something a little skater boy might zoom around in. This modern silhouette features a long length and slim, sporty fit. The squishy, extrafine DK-weight merino yarn strikes just the right balance of softness, warmth, and breathability—for a pullover perfect indoors and out.

materials

- Debbie Bliss Rialto DK, 100% extrafine merino wool, 1¾ oz (50g), 115 yd (105m); 3 (4, 4, 5, 5, 5) balls in #12 Red (MC), 3 (3, 4, 4, 4, 5) balls in #18 Blue (CC) (3)
- Size U.S. 5 (3.75mm) circular needle, 16" (40.5cm) length, or size to obtain gauge
- Size U.S. 5 (3.75mm) double-pointed needles for sleeves
- Size U.S. 4 (3.5mm) double-pointed needles
- Size U.S. 4 (3.5mm) circular needle, 16" (40.5cm) length
- 4 stitch markers (3 of color A and 1 of color B)
- 2 stitch holders
- Darning needle

gauge

5¾ stitches and 8 rounds = 1" (2.5cm) in stockinette stitch

notes

To knit the Stripe pattern: Work 16 rows/rounds in MC and then 16 rows/rounds in CC.
Repeat these 32 rows/rounds for the stripe pattern.
Refer to Special Stitches and Techniques (page 151) for instructions on the k1, p1 rib, and backward-loop cast-on.

skill level
Easy

sizes
2 (4, 6, 8, 10, 12) years.
Shown in size 4.

finished measurements
Chest circumference: 22 (23¼, 26, 27½, 28, 30¼)" (56 [59, 66, 70, 71, 76.5]cm)
Length: 14¾ (16¼, 17¾, 19¼, 20, 21)" (37.5 [41, 45, 49, 51, 53.5]cm)

YOKE

With the larger needle and MC, cast on 2 (2, 3, 4, 4, 4) front stitches, place a marker A, cast on 10 (10, 10, 12, 14, 14) sleeve stitches, place a marker A, cast on 27 (29, 31, 33, 35, 37) back stitches, place a marker B, cast on 10 (10, 10, 12, 14, 14) sleeve stitches, place a marker A, cast on 2 (2, 3, 4, 4, 4) front stitches—51 (53, 57, 65, 71, 73) stitches.

Increase row (RS): Knit into the front and back of the stitch (kfb), *knit to 1 stitch before the marker, kfb, slip the marker, kfb; repeat from * 3 times more, knit to the last stitch, kfb (10 stitches increased).

Continue working in stockinette stitch in MC, repeating the Increase row every right-side row 7 times, ending with a right-side row. Using the backward-loop cast-on, cast on 7 (9, 9, 9, 11, 13) stitches at the end of the last row—138 (142, 146, 154, 162, 166) stitches.

Join for working in the round and knit to marker B. Change to CC to work in Stripe pattern at this new beginning of round.

Raglan Increase round: [Slip the marker, kfb, knit to marker, kfb] 4 times (8 stitches increased).

Repeat Raglan Increase round every other round 2 (2, 5, 5, 4, 6) times more, then every 4 rounds 5 (6, 6, 7, 8, 8) times—202 (214, 242, 258, 266, 286) stitches.

divide for body and sleeves

Note: Increase stitches by using the backward-loop cast-on.

K59 (63, 71, 75, 77, 83) back stitches, cast on 4 stitches, place 42 (44, 50, 54, 56, 60) sleeve stitches on a holder, k59 (63, 71, 75, 77, 83) front stitches, cast on 4 stitches, and place the remaining 42 (44, 50, 54, 56, 60) sleeve stitches on a holder—126 (134, 150, 158, 162, 174) body stitches.

BODY

Continue in the Stripe pattern until the body measures 8 (9, 10, 11, 11½, 12)" (20.5 [23, 25.5, 28, 29.5, 30.5]cm) from the underarm.

Change to smaller needles and MC; knit 1 round. Work in k1, p1 rib for 1¼" (3cm). Bind off loosely in rib.

SLEEVES (*make 2*)

Place 42 (44, 50, 54, 56, 60) sleeve stitches onto double-pointed needles.

Cast on 2 stitches, k42 (44, 50, 54, 56, 60) sleeve stitches, cast on 2 stitches—46 (48, 54, 58, 60, 64) stitches.

Continue in the Stripe pattern as established until the sleeve measures 4 (6, 7, 8, 9, 10½)" (10 [15, 18, 20.5, 23, 26.5]cm) from the underarm.

Decrease round: K1, k2tog, knit to the last 2 stitches, ssk (2 stitches decreased).

Continue in Stripe pattern, repeating the Decrease round every 8 rounds 3 times more, then work even until the sleeve measures 8½ (10½, 11½, 12½, 13½, 15)" (21.5 [26.5, 29.5, 32, 34.5, 38]cm) from underarm—38 (40, 46, 50, 52, 56) stitches remain.

Change to smaller needles and MC; knit 1 round. Work in k1, p1 rib for 1¼" (3cm). Bind off loosely in rib.

NECK BAND

With the right side facing you, the smaller needles, and MC, start at the back right shoulder and pick up and knit 26 (26, 26, 28, 30, 30) stitches across the back neck, pick up and knit 10 (10, 10, 12, 14, 14) stitches across the top of the left sleeve, pick up and knit 34 (36, 36, 36, 38, 40) stitches across the front neck, and 10 (10, 10, 12, 14, 14) stitches across the top of the right sleeve—80 (82, 82, 88, 96, 98) stitches.

Work in k1, p1 rib in the round for 1¼" (3cm). Bind off loosely in rib.

FINISHING

Sew the underarm seams. Weave in the ends. Block, if desired.

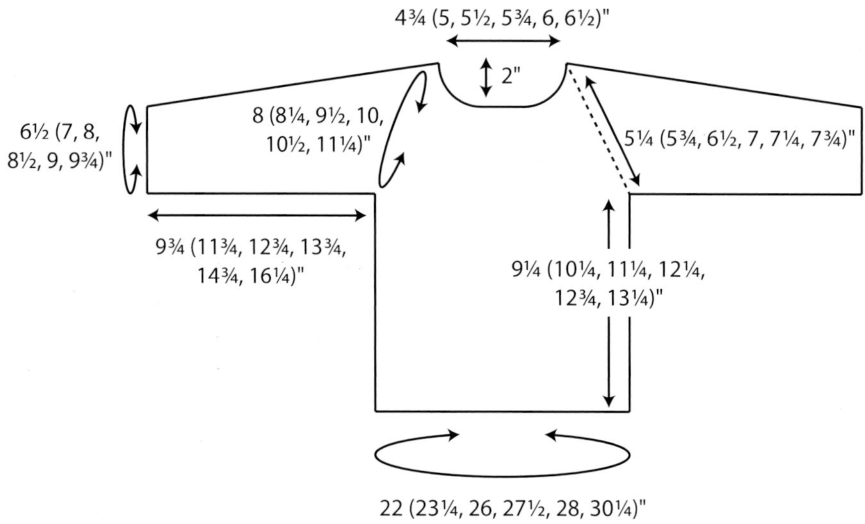

aiden doll pullover

skill level

Easy

finished measurement

Chest circumference: 11–13" (28–33cm)

materials

- Debbie Bliss Rialto DK, 100% extrafine merino wool, 1¾ oz (50g), 115 yd (105m); 1 ball each in #12 Scarlet (MC) and #35 Royal Blue (CC) (3)
- Size U.S. 5 (3.75mm) circular needle 16" (40.5cm) for Magic Loop method, or size to obtain gauge
- Size U.S. 5 (3.75mm) double-pointed needles for sleeves
- Size U.S. 4 (3.5mm) double-pointed needles
- 4 stitch markers
- 2 stitch holders
- Darning needle
- 3 buttons, ½" (13mm)

gauge

5¾ stitches and 8 rounds = 1" (2.5cm) in stockinette stitch

notes

To knit the Stripe pattern: Work 8 rows/rounds in MC and then 8 rows/rounds in CC. Repeat these 16 rows/rounds for the Stripe pattern.

Refer to Special Stitches and Techniques (page 151) for instructions on the k1, p1 rib, Magic Loop method, and backward-loop cast-on.

BODY

With larger needle and MC, cast on 8 stitches, place a marker, cast on 2 stitches, place a marker, cast on 18 stitches, place a marker, cast on 2 stitches, place a marker, cast on 8 stitches—38 stitches.

Work 3 rows in k1, p1 rib.

Increase row (RS): With CC, *knit to 1 stitch before the marker, kfb, slip the marker, kfb; repeat from * 3 times more, knit to the end (8 stitches increased).

Next row: Purl.

Repeat the last two rows 11 times more, making sure to continue in the Stripe pattern—134 stitches.

divide for body and sleeves

Note: Increase stitches by using the backward-loop cast-on.

K20 front stitches, cast on 6 stitches, place 26 sleeve stitches on a holder, k42 back stitches, cast on 6 stitches, place 26 sleeve stitches on a holder, and k20 front stitches—94 body stitches.

Continue in the Stripe pattern as established until the body measures 2½" (6.5cm) from the underarm.

Change to the smaller needles and MC; knit 1 round. Work 3 rows in k1, p1 rib. Bind off loosely in rib.

SLEEVES (*make 2*)

Place 26 sleeve stitches onto larger needles. Cast on 3 stitches, k26 sleeve stitches, cast on 3 stitches—32 stitches. Place a marker and join for working in the round.

Continue in the Stripe pattern as established until the sleeve measures 3" (7.5cm) from the underarm.

Change to the smaller needles and MC; knit 1 round. Work k1, p1 rib for ½" (13mm). Bind off loosely in rib.

BUTTONHOLE BAND

With the right side facing, smaller needles, and MC, start at the neck edging and pick up and knit 32 stitches along the back right opening.

Row 1 (WS): *K1, p1; repeat from * to end.

Row 2: *[K1, p1] twice, yarn over, p2tog; repeat from * twice more, continue in rib as established to the end.

Row 3: Repeat row 1.

Bind off in rib.

BUTTON BAND

With the right side facing, smaller needles, and MC, start at the bottom corner and pick up and knit 32 stitches along the back left opening.

Rows 1–3: *K1, p1; repeat from * to end.

Bind off in rib.

FINISHING

Sew the buttons to the button band opposite the buttonholes.

Sew the underarm seams. Weave in the ends. Block, if desired.

ari owl sweater

I designed this Fair Isle owl pattern using my tablet device, sharing various iterations with good knitting friends, tweaking the little design stitch by stitch until it looked just right. My youngest daughter loves owls, and I knit this sweater's gauge swatch into a coordinating little owl hat just for her (Rowan Owl Hat, page 128).

skill level
Intermediate

sizes
1 (2, 3, 4, 5, 6) years.
Shown in size 2.

finished measurements
Chest circumference:
20 (22, 23½, 25, 26, 27)" (51 [56, 59.5, 63.5, 66, 68.5]cm)
Length 11½ (12½, 13½, 14½, 15, 15¾)" (29.5 [32, 34.5, 37, 38, 40]cm)

materials

- Lorna's Laces Shepherd Worsted, 100% superwash merino wool, 4 oz (114g), 225 yd (206m); 2 (2, 2, 3, 3, 4) skeins in Natural (A), 100 yd (91m) each in Harvest (B), Solitude (C), Fjord (D), and Navy (E) 4
- Size U.S. 7 (4.5mm) circular needle, 24" (61cm) length for body, or size to obtain gauge
- Size U.S. 7 (4.5mm) double-pointed needles for sleeves
- Size U.S. 7 (4.5mm) circular needle, 12" (30.5cm) length for yoke
- Size U.S. 6 (4mm) circular needle, 24" (61cm) length
- Stitch marker
- 6 stitch holders
- Darning needle

gauge

5 stitches and 6 rows = 1" (2.5cm) in stockinette stitch in the round
5 stitches and 6 rows = 1" (2.5cm) in stockinette stitch in Fair Isle in the round

notes

Refer to Special Stitches and Techniques (page 151) for instructions on the k1, p1 rib, and grafting stitches.
If using Lorna's Laces Shepherd Worsted yarn, I do not recommend machine drying after washing. Although it is a superwash merino wool yarn, the heat may affect the two-color rounds differently from the rest of the sweater and may distort the design.

Special Stitch

Corrugated rib

Round 1: *K1 A, p1 B; repeat from * around.

tip: If you tend to knit Fair Isle at a tighter gauge than usual, use 1 needle size larger on the Fair Isle motif.

BODY

With A and smaller needle, cast on 100 (110, 118, 124, 130, 136) stitches. Place a marker and join for working in the round.

Round 1: *K1, p1, repeat from * to the end.

Rounds 2–7 (Corrugated rib): *K1 in A, p1 in B; repeat from * around.

Next round: Change to larger needle and work even in stockinette stitch with A until piece measures 6½ (7½, 8, 8½, 9, 9½)" (16.5 [19, 20.5, 21.5, 23, 24]cm) from the cast-on edge.

divide body and underarms

Next round: [Place the next 42 (45, 49, 52, 55, 58) stitches onto a holder for the body, place the following 8 (10, 10, 10, 10, 10) stitches onto a holder for underarm] twice. Four stitch holders used. Put this piece aside.

SLEEVES *(make 2)*

With A and smaller needles, cast on 42 (44, 46, 48, 48, 50) stitches.

Round 1: *K1, p1, repeat from * to the end.

Rounds 2–7 (Corrugated rib): *K1 with A, p1 with B; repeat from * around.

Next round: Change to larger double-pointed needles and work even in stockinette stitch with A until piece measures 7 (9, 9¾, 10½, 11¼, 11¾)" (18 [23, 25, 26.5, 28.5, 30]cm) from the cast-on edge. Place the last 8 (10, 10, 10, 10) stitches onto a holder—34 (34, 36, 38, 38, 40) stitches remain.

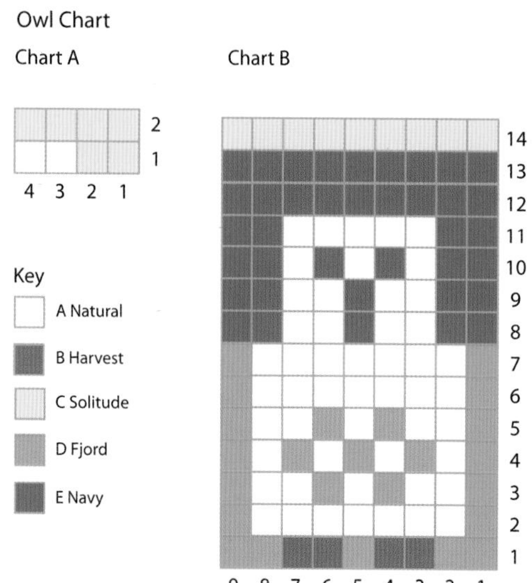

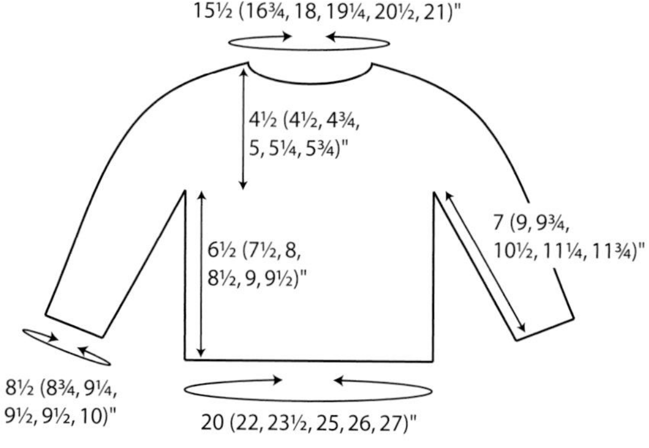

YOKE

Joining round: Place a marker for the beginning of the round. Pick up and knit from stitch holders. [k42 (45, 49, 52, 55, 58) body stitches, k34 (34, 36, 38, 38, 40) sleeve stitches] twice—152 (158, 170, 180, 186, 196) stitches.

Work even in stockinette stitch for 1" (2.5cm).

Size 1 Only

K3, k2tog, k2, k2tog, *k3, k2tog, [k2, k2tog] twice; repeat from * around—117 stitches.

Size 2 Only

*K2, k2tog, [k3, k2tog] 15 times; repeat from * once more—126 stitches.

Size 3 Only

*K2, k2tog, [k3, k2tog] 6 times; repeat from * around—135 stitches.

Size 4 Only

*K3, k2tog; repeat from * around—144 stitches.

Size 5 Only

[K3, k2tog] twice, *[k4, k2tog] twice, k3, k2tog; repeat from * to the last 6 stitches, k4, k2tog—153 stitches.

Size 6 Only

[K4, k2tog] twice, *k3, k2tog, [k4, k2tog] 3 times; repeat from * around—162 stitches.

All Sizes

Work rounds 1–2 of Chart A, ending with stitch 1 (2, 3, 4, 1, 2), then rounds 1–12 of Chart B.

Decrease round; With C, *k1, k2tog; repeat from * around—78 (84, 90, 96, 102, 108) stitches.

Next round: Work round 14 of Chart B

Work 3 (3, 4, 6, 8, 10) rounds even with A.

Change to the smaller needles and work 4 rounds in corrugated rib. Bind off in pattern.

FINISHING

Graft underarm stitches together. Weave in long ends, as superwash merino tends to slip out a bit from wear and washing.

PLAYING FAVORITES

Some children are territorial over their favorite toys, and some aren't quite as attached. My four-year-old never had a "lovey," or security blanket, or a can't-sleep-without-it dolly. In fact, the key to potty training her was bribing her with a princess dress. Who can account for a child's taste? I always brace for disappointment when I show my children the new doll I'm excited about; sometimes it's best to own up to the fact that I might be living a little vicariously through them. I intend to eventually get my daughter a very nice toy horse collection, for example. Back when I was growing up, a realistic-looking toy horse was surprisingly hard to come by. If she doesn't like playing with them, I just might have to!

ari doll owl sweater

skill level

Intermediate

finished measurement

Chest circumference: 11–13" (28–33cm)

materials

- Lorna's Laces Shepherd Worsted, 100% superwash merino wool, 4 oz (114g), 225 yd (206m); 100 yd (91m) in Natural (A), 50 yd (46m) each in Harvest (B), Solitude (C), Fjord (D), and Navy (E) 4
- Size U.S. 7 (4.5mm) double-pointed needles, or circular needle for Magic Loop method, or size to obtain gauge
- Stitch marker
- 6 stitch holders
- Darning needle

gauge

5 stitches and 6 rows = 1" (2.5cm) in stockinette stitch

notes

To make size adjustments, cast on 9 fewer, or more, stitches to accommodate the owl pattern repeat, which is 9 stitches wide and measures almost 2 inches (5cm). Making a sleeve length adjustment is an easier change: Just knit each sleeve a bit longer or shorter before joining to the sweater body.

Refer to Special Stitches and Techniques (page 151) for instructions on the k1, p1 rib, Magic Loop method, and grafting stitches.

If using Lorna's Laces Shepherd Worsted yarn, I do not recommend machine drying after washing. Although it is a superwash merino wool yarn, the heat may affect the two-color rounds differently from the rest of the sweater and may distort the design.

special stitch

Corrugated rib

Round 1: *K1 A, p1 B; repeat from * around.

---

tip: Achieving consistent tension in Fair Isle is something to strive for, but not always possible, especially when knitting small projects. If your Fair Isle band looks too tight (or too loose), block it after each wash for a smoother finish.

BODY

With A, cast on 72 stitches. Place a marker and join for working in the round.

Round 1: *K1, p1, repeat from * to the end.

Rounds 2–4 (corrugated rib): *K1 with A, p1 with B; repeat from * around.

Rounds 5 and 6: With A, work even in stockinette stitch.

Round 7: Work round 1 of Owl Chart A.

Rounds 8–21: Work rounds 1–14 of Owl Chart B.

Rounds 22 and 23: With A, work even in stockinette stitch.

divide body and underarms

Next round: Place the next 15 stitches onto a holder for the body, place the following 6 stitches onto a holder for underarm, place the next 30 stitches onto a holder for the body, place the following 6 stitches onto a holder for the underarm, place the remaining 15 stitches onto a holder and set aside.

SLEEVES (*make two*)

With A, cast on 30 stitches. Place a marker and join for working in the round.

Round 1: *K1, p1, repeat from * to end.

Rounds 2–4 (Corrugated rib): *K1 with A, p1 with B; repeat from * around.

Next round: With A, work even in stockinette stitch until sleeve measures 3" (7.5cm) from the cast-on edge. Place the last 6 stitches on a holder.

YOKE

Note: Joining the body and sleeves sections in the round to work the yoke can be a bit tricky on such a small scale, but with a little perseverance it can be done. This is the hardest part of this sweater construction but everything else knits so quickly that it is worth it!

Joining round: K15 body stitches, k24 sleeve stitches, k30 body stitches, k24 sleeve stitches, k15 body stitches—108 stitches. Place a marker to indicate the beginning of the round.

Rounds 2–4: Work even in stockinette stitch.

Note: To complete the yoke, turn your work. The sweater will be worked flat instead of in the round.

Row 1 (WS): P108.
Row 2: *K2, k2tog; repeat from * to end—72 stitches remain.
Rows 3, 5, and 7: Purl.
Rows 4 and 6: Knit.
Row 8: *K2, k2tog; repeat from * to end—48 stitches remain.
Row 9: K1, p1, yarn over, k2tog, *p1, k1; repeat from * to end.
Rows 10 and 11: Work in k1, p1 rib as established.
Bind off in pattern.

FINISHING

Graft underarm stitches together leaving long ends, as superwash merino tends to slip out from wear and washing. Weave in the ends. Block, if desired.

gigi military jacket

Many of our family members have a military background or other jobs that require uniforms. My kids love to see their uncles and grown-up cousins in their special clothes. I used the tailoring and details common to uniforms, such as epaulets and chevrons, while incorporating a kid-friendly, funky pop of color in this whimsical jacket with grown-up style.

materials

- Lorna's Laces Shepherd Worsted 100% superwash merino wool, 4 oz (114g), 225 yd (206m); 3 (4, 4, 5, 5) skeins in Poppy (4)
- Size U.S. 7 (4.5mm) circular needle, 24" (61cm) length or longer, or size to obtain gauge
- Size U.S. 5 (3.75mm) circular needle, 24" (61cm) length or longer
- Size U.S. F/5 (3.75mm) crochet hook
- 2 stitch markers
- 4 stitch holders
- 6 buttons, 1 1/16" (2.7cm)
- 4 sets of two-piece snaps
- Darning needle

gauge

5 stitches and 7 rows = 1" (2.5cm) in stockinette stitch

notes

This jacket is knit from the bottom up with the body worked in one piece. The sleeves are worked flat from the cuff up.

Refer to Special Stitches and Techniques (page 151) for instructions on the three-needle bind-off and single crochet.

skill level

Advanced

sizes

1 (2, 4, 6, 8) years.
Shown in size 2.

finished measurements

Chest circumference: 22 1/2 (23 1/2, 24 1/4, 25 3/4, 27 1/2)" (57.5 [59.5, 61.5, 65.5, 70] cm), buttoned

Length: 12 1/2 (14 1/2, 15 3/4, 17 1/2, 18 3/4)" (32 [37, 40, 44.5, 47.5]cm)

BODY

With smaller needle, cast on 147 (152, 157, 167, 177) stitches.

Rows 1-7: Knit.

Row 8 (WS): K5, purl to 5 stitches from the end, k5.

Row 9: Knit.

Repeat rows 8 and 9 until body measures 3½ (4, 4½, 5, 5½)" (9 [10, 11.5, 12.5, 14]cm) from the cast-on edge, ending with a wrong-side row.

Decrease row (RS): K5, [k2tog, k2] 3 times, [k2tog, k3] 23 (24, 25, 27, 29) times, [k2tog, k2] twice, k2tog, k5–118 (122, 126, 134, 142) stitches remain.

Next row: K5, purl to 5 stitches from the end, k5.

Next row (RS): K34 (35, 36, 38, 41), place a marker for right side seam, k56 (58, 60, 64, 68), place a marker for left side seam, k28 (29, 30, 32, 33).

Work even in pattern as established until body measures 8 (9, 10, 11, 12)" (20.5 [23, 25.5, 28, 30.5]cm) from the cast-on edge, ending with a wrong-side row.

divide for fronts and back

Next row (RS): *Knit to 7 (5, 5, 6, 6) stitches before side marker, bind off the next 14 (10, 10, 12, 12) stitches; repeat from * once more, knit to the end.

Place 27 (30, 31, 32, 35) right front and 42 (48, 50, 52, 56) back stitches onto holders.

LEFT FRONT

Starting with a wrong-side row, continue in pattern on 21 (24, 25, 26, 27) stitches as established until armhole measures 3 (3¾, 4¼, 4¾, 5¼)" (7.5 [9.5, 11, 12, 13]cm), ending with a right-side row.

shape neck

Row 1 (WS): Bind off 3 (3, 3, 3, 3) stitches, purl to the end.

Rows 2 and 4: Knit.

Row 3: Bind off 3 (3, 3, 3, 4) stitches, purl to the end.

Row 5: Bind off 3 (4, 3, 4, 4) stitches, purl to the end–12 (14, 16, 16, 16) stitches.

Work even in stockinette stitch until armhole measures 4½ (5½, 6, 6½, 7)" (11.5 [14, 15, 16.5, 18]cm).

Place shoulder stitches onto a holder.

BACK

Place back stitches onto larger needle, ready to work a wrong-side row, and join yarn.

Work even in stockinette stitch until the back measures 4¼ (5, 5½, 6, 6½)" (11 [12.5, 14, 15, 16.5]cm) from the underarm, ending with a wrong-side row.

shape back neck

Next row (RS): K12 (14, 16, 16, 16)), place the center 18 (20, 18, 20, 24) stitches on a holder. Join a second ball of yarn and k12 (14, 16, 16, 16).

Working both shoulders at the same time, continue in stockinette stitch until the armhole measures 4½ (5½, 6, 6½, 7)" (11.5 [14, 15, 16.5, 18]cm).

Place stitches from both shoulders onto holders.

RIGHT FRONT

Place right front stitches onto larger needles, ready to work a wrong-side row, and join yarn.

Next row (WS): Purl to last 5 stitches, k5.

Continue in stockinette stitch until armhole measures 3 (3¾, 4¼, 4¾, 5¼)" (7.5 [9.5, 11, 12, 13]cm), ending with a wrong-side row.

shape neck

Row 1 (RS): Bind off 5 (5, 5, 5, 6) stitches, knit to the end.

Rows 2 and 4: Purl.

Row 3: Bind off 5 (5, 5, 5, 6) stitches, knit to the end.

Row 5: Bind off 5 (6, 5, 6, 7) stitches, knit to the end—12 (14, 16, 16, 16) stitches.

Work even until armhole measures 4½ (5½, 6, 6½, 7)" (11.5 [14, 15, 16.5, 18]cm).

Place shoulder stitches onto a holder.

SLEEVES (*make 2*)

With smaller needles, cast on 34 (34, 34, 36, 36) stitches.

Rows 1-6: Knit.

Change to larger needles.

Left Sleeve Only

Setup row (RS): K2, place a marker, work 19 stitches of Sleeve Chevron pattern, place a marker, knit to the end.

Right Sleeve Only

Setup row (RS): K13 (13, 13, 15, 15), place a marker, work 19 stitches of Sleeve Chevron pattern, place a marker, k2.

Both Sleeves

Continue in stockinette stitch, working Sleeve Chevron pattern between markers, until 12 rows of the chart are complete.

sleeve shaping

Note: Create m1 increases by picking up the bar between the stitches to be knit and then knitting into the back loop.

Increase row (RS): K2, m1, work in pattern as established to the last 2 stitches, m1, k2 (2 stitches increased).

Continuing in pattern as established, working chart between markers until complete, repeat Increase row every 4 (4, 6, 6, 6) rows 5 (6, 7, 7, 9) times more—46 (48, 50, 52, 56) stitches.

Work even in stockinette stitch until sleeve measures 7 (9, 11, 12, 13)" (18 [23, 28, 30.5, 33] cm) from the cast-on edge.

shape sleeve cap

Bind off 7 (5, 5, 6, 6) stitches at the beginning of the next 2 rows—32 (38, 40, 40, 44) stitches remain.

Decrease row (RS): K1, ssk, knit to the last 3 stitches, k2tog, k1 (2 stitches decreased).

Repeat Decrease row every right-side row 10

(13, 14, 14, 16) times more—10 stitches remain. Bind off.

HOOD

Place left front and back shoulder stitches onto two needles. With right sides together, join shoulder stitches using a three-needle bind-off. Join the right shoulder in the same manner.

With right side facing and larger needle, start at the right front neck and pick up and knit 52 (60, 56, 60, 68) stitches evenly around the neck opening.

Increase row (WS): P3 (2, 2, 3, 3), purl through the front and back of the next stitch (pfb), [p1, pfb] 0 (1, 12, 8, 0) times, [p2, pfb] 0 (17, 1, 7, 4) times, [p3, pfb] 11 (0, 0, 0, 9) times, [p2, pfb] 0 (0, 0, 0, 4) times, [p1, pfb] 0 (1, 12, 8, 0) times, p4 (2, 2, 3, 4)—64 (80, 82, 84, 86) stitches.

Row 1 (RS): With yarn in back, slip 2 stitches, then work 13 stitches of the Hood Chevron pattern, place a marker, knit to the last 15 stitches, place a marker, work the 13 stitches of the Hood Chevron pattern, slip 2 stitches with yarn in back.

Row 2: P2, work the 13 stitches of the pattern, purl to the marker, work 13 stitches of pattern, p2.

Repeat rows 1 and 2 until hood measures 9 (10, 10½, 11, 12)" (23 [25.5, 26.5, 28, 30.5]cm) from pickup row.

Place half the stitches on each of two needles, fold the hood in half with right sides together, and close the top of the hood using the three-needle bind-off.

BUTTON TABS (*make 3*)

With smaller needles, cast on 8 stitches. Work in stockinette stitch until the tab measures 3¼" (8cm). Bind off.

Work one round of single crochet around the tab.

FINISHING

Set the sleeves into armholes. Sew sleeve seams.

Sew the buttons onto the button tabs. Sew the button tabs onto the right front.

Sew the snaps along the edges of the front opening.

Weave in the ends and block.

Hood Chevron Pattern

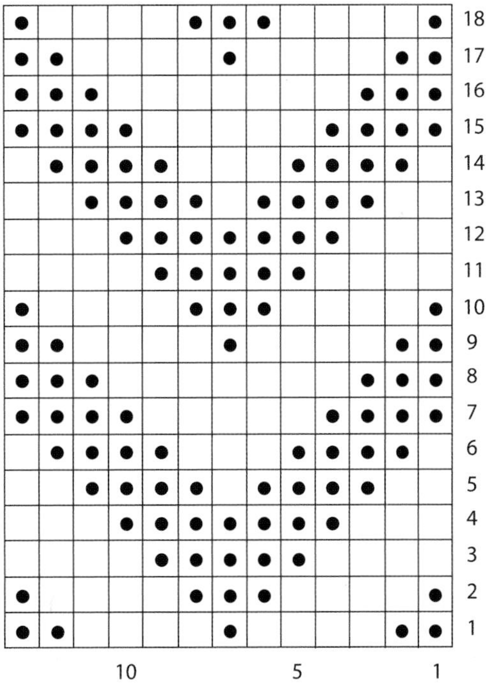

●					●	●	●					●	18
●	●					●					●	●	17
●	●	●								●	●	●	16
●	●	●	●						●	●	●	●	15
	●	●	●	●				●	●	●	●		14
		●	●	●	●		●	●	●	●			13
			●	●	●	●	●	●	●				12
				●	●	●	●	●					11
●					●	●	●					●	10
●	●					●					●	●	9
●	●	●								●	●	●	8
●	●	●	●						●	●	●	●	7
	●	●	●	●				●	●	●	●		6
		●	●	●	●		●	●	●	●			5
			●	●	●	●	●	●	●				4
				●	●	●	●	●					3
●					●	●	●					●	2
●	●					●					●	●	1
			10					5				1	

Sleeve Chevron Pattern

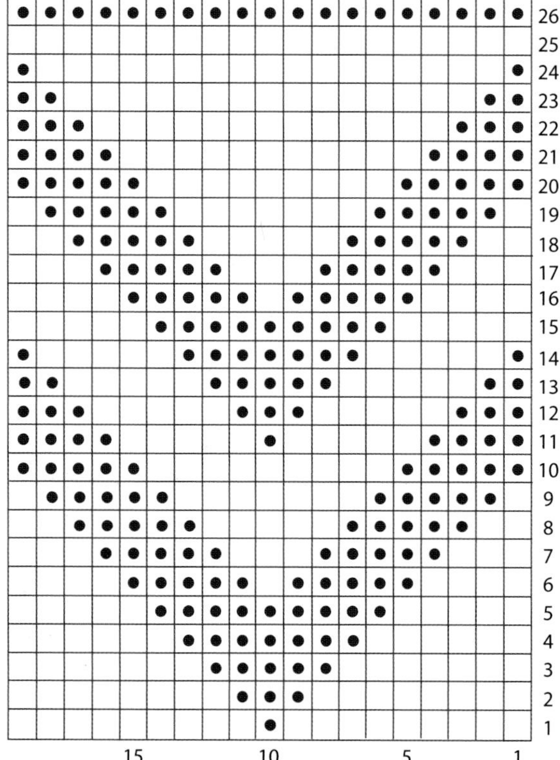

Key

RS: knit
WS: purl

WS: purl
RS: knit

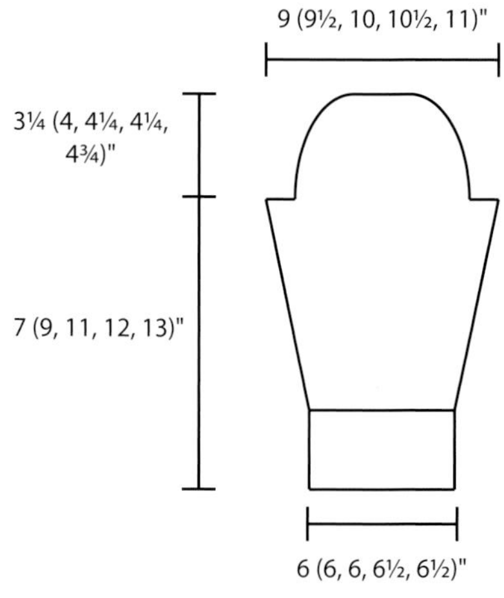

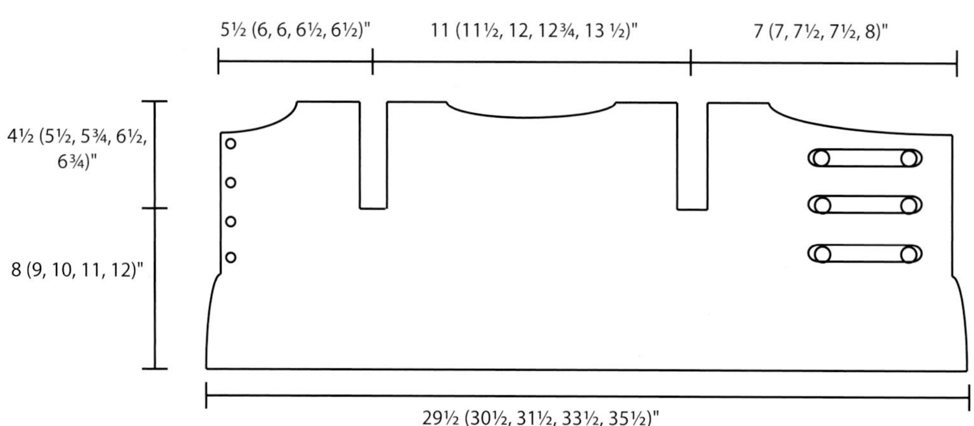

gigi doll military jacket

skill level

Advanced

finished measurement

Chest circumference: 11–13" (28–33cm)

materials

- Lorna's Laces Shepherd Worsted, 100% superwash merino wool, 4 oz (114g), 225 yd (206m); 1 skein in Poppy (4)
- Size U.S. 7 (4.5mm) circular needle, 24" (61cm) length, or size to obtain gauge
- Size U.S. 5 (3.75mm) circular needle, 24" (61cm) length
- Size U.S. F/5 (3.75mm) crochet hook
- 4 stitch holders
- 2 stitch markers
- 4 buttons, 7/8" (2.1cm)
- 2 sets of two-piece snaps
- Darning needle

gauge

5 stitches and 7 rows = 1" (2.5cm) in stockinette stitch

notes

This jacket is knit from the bottom up with the body worked in one piece. The sleeves are worked flat from the cuff up. Refer to Special Stitches and Techniques (page 151) for instructions on the three-needle bind-off, grafting stitches, and single crochet.

BODY

With smaller needle, cast on 80 stitches.

Rows 1-5: Knit.

Change to larger needles.

Row 6 (WS): K3, purl to 3 stitches from the end, k3.

Row 7: Knit.

Repeat rows 6 and 7 until body measures 2" (5cm) from the cast-on edge, ending with a wrong-side row.

Decrease row (RS): *K8, k2tog; repeat from * to the last 10 stitches, k5, k2tog, k3—72 stitches remain.

Next row: K3, purl to 3 stitches from the end, k3.

Next row: Knit.

Work even as established until body measures 3½" (9cm) from the cast-on edge, ending with a wrong-side row.

divide for fronts and back

Next row (RS): *K22, bind off the next 4 stitches, k30, bind off the next 4 stitches, k12.

Place 22 right front and 30 back stitches onto holders.

LEFT FRONT

Starting with a wrong-side row, continue in pattern as established on 22 stitches until armhole measures 2" (5cm), ending with a right-side row.

shape neck

Row 1 (WS): Bind off 3 stitches, purl to the end.

Row 2: Knit.

Row 3: Bind off 13 stitches, purl to the end—6 stitches remain.

Work even in stockinette stitch until armhole measures 3" (7.5cm).

Place shoulder stitches onto a holder.

BACK

Place back stitches onto larger needle, ready to work a wrong-side row, and join yarn.

Work even in stockinette stitch until the back measures 3" (7.5cm) from the underarm, ending with a wrong-side row.

Next row (RS): K6 and place these stitches on a holder, bind off the center 18 stitches, k6, and place these stitches on a holder.

RIGHT FRONT

Place right front stitches onto larger needle, ready to work a wrong-side row, and join yarn.

Next row (WS): Purl to last 3 stitches, k3.

Continue in pattern as established until armhole measures 2" (5cm), ending with a wrong-side row.

shape neck

Row 1 (RS): Bind off 3 stitches, knit to the end—9 stitches remain.

Row 2: Purl.

Row 3: Bind off 3 stitches, knit to the end—6 stitches remain.

Work even in stockinette stitch until armhole measures 3" (7.5cm).

Place shoulder stitches onto a holder and set this piece aside.

SLEEVES (*make 2*)

With smaller needles, cast on 40 stitches.

Rows 1–6: Knit 6 rows.

Change to larger needles.

Starting with a knit row, work even in stockinette stitch until sleeve measures 3" (7.5cm) from the cast-on edge.

Bind off.

HOOD

Place left front and back shoulder stitches onto two needles. With right sides together, join shoulder stitches using a three-needle bind-off. Join the right shoulder in the same manner.

With right side facing and larger needle, start at the right front neck and pick up and knit 32 stitches evenly around neck opening.

Rows 1 and 3: K3, purl to 3 stitches before the end, k3.

Row 2: K15, place a marker, k2, place a marker, k15.

Increase row: Knit to 1 stitch before the marker, kfb, slip the marker, k2, slip the marker, kfb, knit to the end (2 stitches increased).

Continue in pattern as established, repeat Increase row every right-side row 11 times more—56 stitches.

Work 6 rows even in pattern.

Decrease row: Knit to 2 stitches before the marker, ssk, slip the marker, k2, slip the marker, k2tog, knit to the end (2 stitches decreased).

Continue in pattern as established, repeat Decrease row every right-side row twice more—50 stitches remain.

Repeat row 1.

Place half the stitches on each of the two needles, fold the hood in half with right sides together, and graft the top of the hood together.

FAUX BUTTON TABS (*make 2*)

With smaller needles, cast on 6 stitches. Work in stockinette stitch until tab measures 2" (5cm). Bind off.

Work one round of single crochet around the tab.

FINISHING

Set sleeves into armholes. Sew sleeve seams.

Sew 2 buttons onto each faux button tab, then whipstitch the faux button tabs onto the right front.

Sew the snaps along the inside edge of the right front opening, lined up behind the faux button tabs.

Weave in the ends and block.

THE POSSESSED DOLL

As I think back to my childhood, there is one memory in particular, involving my favorite doll, that stands out from all the rest—much to my older sister's chagrin. The doll's name was Cricket, and she was one of the first "talking" dolls, released around the same time as the talking Teddy Ruxpin bears in the mid-eighties. Cricket came with a few cassette tapes that had songs and stories on them. With her white-blond hair, bright-blue eyes, and perky voice, she was the perfect friend for eight-year-old me. At least she was until one afternoon when I turned her on and a husky "monster" voice came out of her mouth! I don't recall what she said that shocked me, but I do remember that Cricket went into my closet and never came out again. Many months later I did take a peek at her, but my perception of Cricket was never the same. You can imagine how angry my mother was at my clever sister for making a recording of herself saying scary things and then sticking that tape into my doll!

My sister and I are three and a half years apart. I never dared touch any of her dolls—or her amazing sticker collection. But when I was sixteen I sneaked into her room and stole a few stickers to put on the bumper of my first car. It wasn't quite fair payback for her Cricket prank, but at least it was some form of justice. Now that I've confessed, I'll just wait and see how much trouble I get into.

reagan pinafore

I've always loved knitting dishcloths—there is something fun about bright cotton that is tough and can withstand a lot of wear and tear. This pinafore was imagined as the perfect gardening frock to help prevent dirt and grass stains from collecting on the clothing underneath. The "dishrag" cotton soaks them up and gives kids a built-in spot to wipe little hands!

materials

- Red Heart Creme de la Creme, 100% cotton, 2½ oz (70.9g), 125½ yd (114.8m);
- 3 (3, 4, 5, 6) skeins in #501 Aqua Jade (MC), 1 (1, 1, 2, 2) skeins in #628 Minty (CC) (4)
- Size U.S. 7 (4.5mm) needles, or size to obtain gauge
- 2 detachable stitch markers
- Stitch holder
- 4 buttons, 1" (2.5cm)
- Darning needle

gauge

5 stitches and 7½ rows = 1" (2.5cm) in stockinette stitch
5 stitches and 7½ rows = 1" (2.5cm) in Pinafore Lace pattern

notes

Refer to Special Stitches and Techniques (page 151) for instructions on the cable cast-on and backward-loop cast-on.

skill level
Intermediate

sizes
2 (4, 6, 8, 10) years.
Shown in size 4 years.

finished measurements
Waist circumference:
20 (23, 24½, 26, 27½)" (51 [58.5, 62, 66, 70]cm), buttoned
Length: 15 (16¾, 19¼, 24¾, 26¼)" (38 [42.5, 49, 63, 66.5]cm)

BACK WAISTBAND

With MC, cast on 10 stitches.

Row 1: *K1, p1; repeat from * to end.

Row 2: *P1, k1; repeat from * to end.

Repeat rows 1 and 2 for seed stitch until the waistband measures 13 (13½, 14¼, 15, 15¾)" (33 [34.5, 36, 38, 40]cm).

Bind off. You may want to knit the last two stitches together before binding off, to create a cleaner edge.

Mark the center 8 (8, 8, 10, 10)" (20.5 [20.5, 20.5, 25.5, 25.5]cm) of the back waistband using two detachable stitch markers.

BACK BIB

With the right side facing and CC, pick up and knit 41 (41, 41, 51, 51) stitches evenly between the markers.

Purl 1 row.

Work the Pinafore Lace pattern as follows:

Row 1: K1, *k2, k2tog, yarn over, k1, yarn over, ssk, k3; repeat from * to end.

Row 2 and all wrong-side rows: Purl.

Row 3: K1, *k1, k2tog [k1, yarn over] twice, k1, ssk, k2; repeat from * to end.

Row 5: K1, *k2tog, k2, yarn over, k1, yarn over, k2, ssk, k1; repeat from * to end.

Row 7: K2tog, *k3, yarn over, k1, yarn over, k3, [slip 1, k2tog, pass slipped stitch over (sk2p)]; repeat from * to last 10 stitches, k3, yarn over, k1, yarn over, k3, ssk.

Row 9: K1, *yarn over, ssk, k5, k2tog, yarn over, k1; repeat from * to end.

Row 11: K1, *yarn over, k1, ssk, k3, k2tog, k1, yarn over, k1; repeat from * to end.

Row 13: K1, *yarn over, k2, ssk, k1, k2tog, k2, yarn over, k1; repeat from * to end.

Row 15: K1, *yarn over, k3, sk2p, k3, yarn over, k1; repeat from * to end.

Row 16: Purl.

Sizes 8 and 10 Only

Repeat rows 1–16.

All Sizes

Repeat rows 1–8.

Work 4 rows in seed stitch.

Bind off, keeping the tension even so that the bib lays flat.

BACK SKIRT

Move the stitch markers to the lower edge of the waistband.

With MC, pick up and knit 72 (72, 72, 90, 90) stitches evenly between markers as follows: *Pick up 1 stitch, cast on 1 stitch using the backward-loop cast-on; repeat from * between markers.

Next row (WS): Purl.

Continue in stockinette stitch until the skirt measures 6½ (7¾, 9¾, 12¾, 13¾)" (16.5 [20, 25, 32.5, 35]cm) from the picked-up edge.

Work 2 rows in seed stitch.

Bind off in pattern, keeping the tension even.

FRONT WAISTBAND

With MC, cast on 10 stitches.

Work 3 rows in seed stitch.

Buttonhole row (RS): Work 3 stitches in seed stitch, bring yarn to the front, slip the next stitch purlwise, then bring the yarn to the back of the work. [Slip the next stitch purlwise and pass the previous slipped stitch over] 4 times. Slip the last stitch back to the left-hand needle.

Next row: Turn the piece so the wrong side is facing and bring the working yarn to the front. Cast on 4 stitches using the cable cast-on (1 stitch more than was bound off), then turn the piece so the right side is facing, with the working yarn at the back. Slip 1 stitch, and pass the previous slipped stitch over; work to the end.

Work 3 rows in seed stitch.

Next row: Repeat the Buttonhole row.

Continue working in seed stitch until the front waistband measures 11¾ (12¼, 13, 13¾, 14½)" (30 [31, 33, 35, 37]cm).

Next row: Repeat the Buttonhole.

Work 3 rows in seed stitch.

Next row: Repeat the Buttonhole row.

Work 3 rows in seed stitch.

Bind off. You may want to knit the last two stitches together before binding them off, to create a cleaner edge.

Mark the center 8 (8, 8, 10, 10)" (20.5 [20.5, 20.5, 25.5, 25.5]cm) of the front waistband using two detachable stitch markers.

FRONT BIB

Work the same as for back bib but do not bind off. Continue as follows:

Next row: K8 and place these stitches on a holder, bind off the center 25 (25, 25, 35, 35) stitches, keeping tension even so that the bib lays flat, and continue in pattern to the end.

SHOULDER STRAP *(make 2)*

Continue in seed stitch on these 8 stitches until strap measures 4¾ (5½, 6½, 7½, 8½)" (12 [14, 16.5, 19, 21.5]cm). Bind off.

Slip the first 8 stitches back onto the needles and work as above.

FRONT SKIRT

Work the same as for the back skirt.

FINISHING

Sew the ends of the shoulder straps to the top of the back bib. Sew the buttons onto the back waistband to correspond with the buttonholes on the front waistband. Weave in the ends.

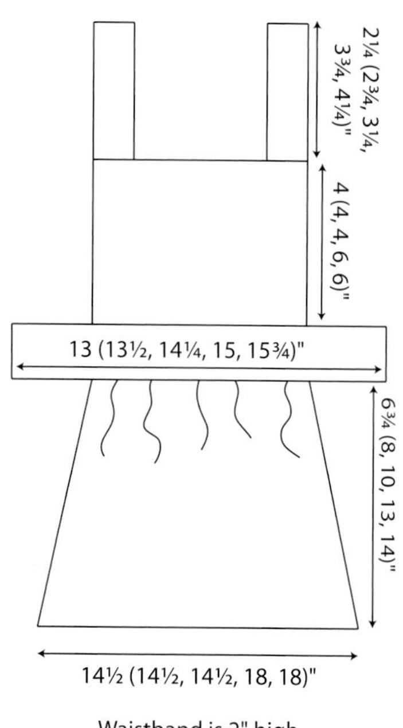

Waistband is 2" high

reagan doll pinafore

skill level

Intermediate

finished measurement

Waist circumference: 11–13" (28–33cm)

materials

- Red Heart Creme de la Creme, 100% cotton, 2½ oz (70.9g), 125½ yd (114.8m); 1 skein each in #501 Aqua Jade (MC) and #628 Minty (CC) (4)
- Size U.S. 7 (4.5mm) needle, or size to obtain gauge
- 2 detachable stitch markers
- Stitch holder
- Darning needle
- 2 buttons, ¾" (2cm)

gauge

5 stitches and 7½ rows = 1" (2.5cm) in stockinette stitch

5 stitches and 7½ rows = 1" (2.5cm) in Pinafore Lace pattern

notes

Refer to Special Stitches and Techniques (page 151) for instructions on the cable cast-on and backward-loop cast-on.

BACK WAISTBAND

With MC, cast on 6 stitches.

Row 1: *K1, p1; repeat from * to end.

Row 2: *P1, k1; repeat from * to end.

Repeat rows 1 and 2 for seed stitch until waistband measures 7½" (19cm).

Bind off. You may want to knit the last two stitches together before binding off, to create a cleaner edge.

Mark the center 4½" (11.5cm) of the back waistband using two detachable stitch markers.

BACK BIB

With right side facing and CC, pick up and knit 21 stitches evenly between markers.

Purl 1 row.

Work the Pinafore Lace pattern as follows:

Row 1: K1, *k2, k2tog, yarn over, k1, yarn over, ssk, k3; repeat from * to end.

Row 2 and all wrong-side rows: Purl.

Row 3: K1, *k1, k2tog [k1, yarn over] twice, k1, ssk, k2; repeat from * to end.

Row 5: K1, *k2tog, k2, yarn over, k1, yarn over, k2, ssk, k1; repeat from * to end.

Row 7: K2tog, k3, yarn over, k1, yarn over, k3, [slip 1, k2tog, pass slipped stitch over (sk2p)]; repeat from * to last 10 stitches, k3, yarn over, k1, yarn over, k3, ssk.

Row 9: K1, *yarn over, ssk, k5, k2tog, yarn over, k1; repeat from * to end.

Row 11: K1, *yarn over, k1, ssk, k3, k2tog, k1, yarn over, k1; repeat from * to end.

Row 13: K1, *yarn over, k2, ssk, k1, k2tog, k2, yarn over, k1; repeat from * to end.

Row 15: K1, *yarn over, k3, sk2p, k3, yarn over, k1; repeat from * to end.

Row 16: Purl.

Work 2 rows in seed stitch.

Bind off in pattern, keeping the tension even so that the bib lies flat.

BACK SKIRT

Move the stitch markers to the lower edge of the waistband.

With MC, pick up and knit 36 stitches evenly between markers as follows: *Pick up 1 stitch, cast on 1 stitch using the backward-loop cast-on; repeat from * between markers.

Next row (WS): Purl.

Continue in stockinette stitch until the skirt measures 3" (7.5cm) from the picked-up edge.

Work 2 rows in seed stitch.

Bind off in pattern, keeping the tension even.

FRONT WAISTBAND

With MC, cast on 6 stitches.

Work 3 rows in seed stitch.

Buttonhole row (RS): Work 2 stitches in pattern, yarn over, k2tog, work 2 stitches in pattern.

Continue working in seed stitch until the waistband measures 7" (18cm), ending with a wrong-side row.

Next row: Repeat Buttonhole row.

Work 3 rows in seed stitch.

Bind off.

Mark the center 4½" (11.5cm) of the front waistband using two detachable stitch markers.

FRONT BIB

With right side facing and CC, pick up and knit 21 stitches evenly between markers.

Purl 1 row.

Work the same as for back bib but do not bind off. Continue as follows:

Next row: K4 and place these stitches onto a holder, bind off center 13 stitches, keeping tension even so the bib lies flat, continue in pattern to end of row.

SHOULDER STRAPS (*make 2*)

Continue in pattern as established on these 4 stitches until the strap measures 3" (7.5cm).

Bind off.

Slip the first 4 stitches back onto the needles and work as above.

FRONT SKIRT

Work the same as for back skirt.

FINISHING

Sew the ends of the straps to the top back bib. Sew the buttons onto the back waistband to correspond with buttonholes on the front waistband. Weave in the ends.

Chapter Two Dress-Up

Getting dressed up is more fun when you've got somewhere to go. Why not plan a tea party at a local park? Bring along the children's lunch, teacups, and their best dolly friends. My girls love it when I unpack small crackers and easy-to-assemble toppings to make little "sandwiches" that they can put together themselves. We fill up their play teapot with something yummy to drink and let the party begin.

The knits in this chapter are all about getting "fancy" and playing dress-up—a ruffled ballet-inspired top for big sister (Satya Ballet Wrap, page 68) or a dashing sweater vest for little brother (Elliot Cabled Vest, page 81). Be sure to snap a few photos for your scrapbook while the little ones are all dressed up.

sydney lace dress

Adapting Elizabeth Zimmermann's Gull Lace pattern (from her Knitter's Almanac***), this dress is a quick-to-knit pattern that keeps your brain working just enough to avoid boredom, but not so hard that you'll want to stop knitting. I chose naturally dyed organic cotton yarns in subtle colors, but this classic stitch will stand up to brighter color combinations as well.***

skill level
Intermediate

sizes
2 (4, 6, 8, 10) years.
Shown in size 4.

finished measurements
Chest circumference: 23¾ (25¼, 26½, 28, 30¾)" (60.5 [64, 67.5, 71, 78]cm)
Length: 21½ (22¾, 25¼, 27¼, 29¼)" (55 [58, 64, 69, 74.5]cm)

materials

- Rowan Purelife Organic Cotton DK, 100% cotton; 1¾ oz (50g), 131 yd (120m); 3 (3, 4, 4, 5) skeins in #994 Medium Indigo (MC), 1 skein in #990 Oak Apple (CC) (3)
- Size U.S. 4 (3.5mm) circular needle, 24" (61cm) length, or size to obtain gauge
- Size U.S. 5 (3.75mm) circular needle, 24" (61cm) length, or size to obtain gauge
- Size U.S. F/5 (3.75mm) crochet hook
- 3 stitch holders
- Stitch marker
- Darning needle
- 1 button, ½" (13mm)

gauge

5 stitches and 10 rows = 1" (2.5cm) in garter stitch on smaller needle
5 stitches and 9 rows = 1" (2.5cm) in Gull Lace on larger needle

special stitch

The Gull Lace pattern is worked flat and in the round. Make sure to purl on rows 2 and 4 when working flat. A chart is provided on page 65.

Row 1 (RS): *K1, k2tog, yarn over, k1, yarn over, ssk, k1; repeat from * to end.
Row 2: Knit.
Row 3: *K2tog, yarn over, k3, yarn over, ssk; repeat from * to end.
Row 4: Knit.

BODY (*in the round*)

Joining round: Continuing in pattern as established, work across back stitches, place front stitches onto needles and work across front stitches. Place a marker and join for working in the round—119 (126, 133, 140, 154) stitches.

Work even in Gull Lace until piece measures 16¾ (17½, 20, 22, 23¼)" (42.5 [44.5, 51, 56, 59]cm) from underarm, ending with row 2.

Note: To accurately measure the piece, fold the dress in half lengthwise and let it hang freely in the air, allowing gravity to naturally weigh down the knit as you measure.

Change to smaller needle and join CC.

Round 1: Knit.

Round 2: Purl.

Repeat rounds 1 and 2 twice more.

Bind off loosely.

FINISHING

Weave in the ends.

BUTTON LOOP

With CC and crochet hook, make a 1½" (3.8cm) chain. Sew the ends of the chain to the top right edge of the yoke, making a button loop. Sew the button to the top left edge, opposite the loop.

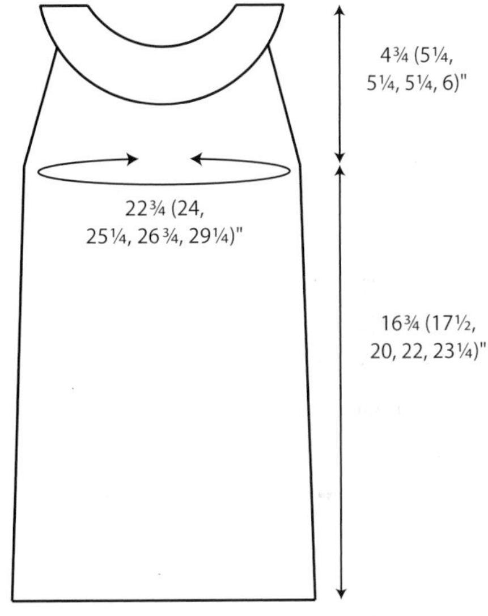

Gull Lace Pattern

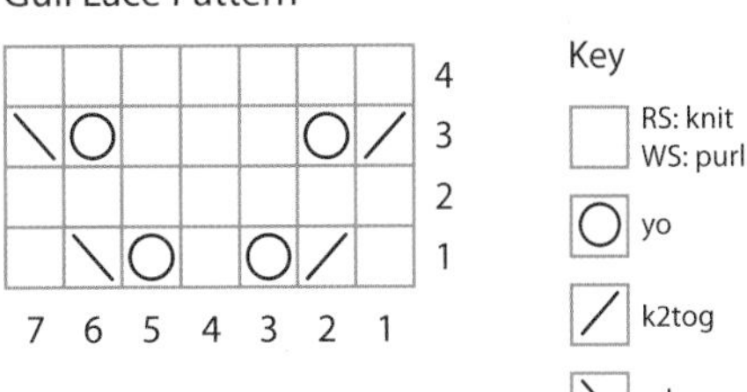

sydney doll lace dress

skill level

Intermediate

finished measurement

Chest circumference: 11–13" (28–33cm)

materials

- Rowan Purelife Organic Cotton DK, 100% cotton, 1¾ oz (50g), 131 yd (120m); 1 skein each in #986 Natural (MC) and #994 Medium Indigo (CC) (3)
- Size U.S. 4 (3.5mm) double-pointed needles, or size to obtain gauge
- Size U.S. 5 (3.75mm) double-pointed needles, or size to obtain gauge
- Size U.S E (3.5mm) crochet hook
- 3 stitch holders
- Stitch marker
- Darning needle
- 1 button, ½" (13mm)

gauge

5 stitches and 10 rows = 1" (2.5cm) in garter stitch on smaller needle

5 stitches and 9 rows = 1" (2.5cm) in Gull Lace on larger needle

notes

The Gull Lace pattern is described on page 62, and appears in chart form on page 65.

M1 using the backward-loop cast-on (page 151).

YOKE

With smaller needles and CC, cast on 45 stitches.

Rows 1-6: Knit.

Row 7 (RS): *K2, m1; repeat from * to the last 3 stitches, k3—66 stitches.

Rows 8 and 9: Knit.

Row 10: *K4, m1; repeat from * to the last 2 stitches, k2—82 stitches.

Row 11: Knit.

Row 12: K14 back stitches and place on a holder, bind off the next 13 shoulder stitches, k28 front stitches, bind off the next 13 shoulder stitches, k14 back stitches and place on a holder.

Cut yarn, leaving a long tail for weaving in.

FRONT

With the right-side facing and larger needles, attach MC.

Row 1: *Knit into the front and back of the stitch (kfb); repeat from * across—56 stitches.

Row 2: Purl.

Rows 3-10: Work rows 1-4 of the Gull Lace pattern (page 65) twice.

Place stitches on a holder. Cut yarn, leaving a tail.

RIGHT BACK

Place stitches onto larger needles, ready to work a right-side row. Attach MC.

Row 1: *Kfb; repeat from * to end—28 stitches.

Row 2: Purl.

Rows 3-10: Work rows 1-4 of the Gull Lace pattern twice.

Cut yarn and place stitches on a holder.

LEFT BACK

Place stitches onto larger needles, ready to work a right-side row. Attach MC.

Work rows 1-10 as for right back. Do not cut yarn.

BODY (*in the round*)

Joining round (RS): Continuing in the pattern as established, work across the left back stitches, place the right back stitches onto needles and work across right back stitches, place the front stitches onto needles and work across front stitches. Place a marker and join for working in the round—112 stitches.

Work even in the Gull Lace pattern until piece measures 4" (10cm) from the underarm, ending with row 2.

Change to the smaller needle and join CC.

Round 1: Knit.

Round 2: Purl.

Repeat rounds 1 and 2 twice more.

Bind off loosely.

FINISHING

Weave in the ends.

BUTTON LOOP

With CC and crochet hook, make a 1½" (3.8cm) long chain. Darn the ends to the top right edge of the yoke. Attach the button to top left edge, opposite the loop.

satya ballet wrap

Why should tutus have all the fun? A cascade of ruffles on each sleeve of this cropped wrap is sure to please the prima ballerina in your life. The ruffle yarn can be a bit tricky to work with; knitting with it on the right side results in ruffles on the wrong side! So work with it every row to create a ruffle inside and out, adding as many, or as few, as your child likes to personalize the design.

skill level
Advanced

sizes
2 (4, 6, 8, 10, 12) years.
Shown in size 6.

finished measurements
Chest width: 10½ (11, 11¾, 12½, 13¼, 14½)" (26.5 [28, 30, 32, 33.5, 37]cm)
Height: 6½ (7½, 8½, 10½, 12, 13)" (16.5 [19, 21.5, 26.5, 30.5, 33]cm)

materials

- Sublime Baby Silk & Bamboo DK, 80% bamboo-sourced viscose, 20% silk; 1¾ oz (50g), 105 yd (96m); 3 (4, 4, 5, 6, 7) balls in #270 (MC) (3)
- Filatura Di Crosa Bandel, 75% cotton, 25% polyamide; 1¾ oz (50g), 77 yd (70m); 1 (1, 1, 2, 2, 2) skeins in #7 Opal (CC)
- Size U.S. 6 (4mm) circular needle, 24" (61cm) length, or size to obtain gauge
- Size U.S. 5 (3.75mm) circular needle, 24" (61cm) length
- 4 stitch markers
- 2 stitch holders or waste yarn
- Darning needle

gauge

5½ stitches and 7½ rows = 1" (2.5cm) in stockinette stitch on larger needle

YOKE

With MC and larger needle, cast on 1 front stitch, place a marker, cast on 8 (8, 8, 8, 8, 7) sleeve stitches, place a marker, cast on 18 (16, 18, 19, 21, 24) back stitches, place a marker, cast on 8 (8, 8, 8, 8, 7) sleeve stitches, place a marker, cast on 1 front stitch—36 (34, 36, 37, 39, 40) stitches.

front neck shaping

Note: Front neck shaping and raglan sleeve shaping are worked *at the same time*. Read through both instructions before starting increases.

RS row: Knit into the front and back of the stitch (kfb), knit to the last stitch, working raglan shaping when required, kfb.

WS row: Purl into the front and back of the stitch (pfb), purl to the last stitch, working raglan shaping when required, pfb.

Work neck shaping increase rows as follows: Starting with the first row (WS), work neck shaping every row 19 (12, 10, 5, 0, 6) times, then every other row 15 (22 27, 37, 45, 46) times—53 (54, 58, 64, 68, 76) front stitches.

raglan sleeve shaping

RS row: *Working neck shaping at each end when required, knit to 1 stitch before the marker, kfb, slip the marker, kfb; repeat from * 3 times more, knit to the end (8 stitches increased).

WS row: *Working neck shaping at each end when required, purl to 1 stitch before the marker, pfb, slip the marker, pfb; repeat from * 3 times more, purl to the end (8 stitches increased).

Work raglan sleeve shaping increase rows as follows: Starting with the second row (RS), work raglan shaping every right-side row 16 (1, 20, 19, 18, 19) times, then every 3 (2, 3, 3, 3, 3) rows 2 (19, 1, 3, 5, 5) times—44 (48, 50, 52, 54, 55) stitches each sleeve, 54 (56, 60, 63, 67, 72) back stitches.

divide sleeves from body

When raglan shaping is complete, ending with a wrong-side row, divide fronts, sleeves, and back.

Continuing neck shaping, work to sleeve marker, cast on 4 (4, 4, 6, 6, 8) stitches, place 44 (48, 50, 52, 54, 55) sleeve stitches on a holder, work 54 (56, 60, 63, 67, 72) back stitches, cast on 4 (4, 4, 6, 6, 8) stitches, place 44 (48, 50, 52, 54, 55) sleeve stitches on a holder, work to end.

Complete neck shaping—168 (174, 186, 205, 217, 242) stitches.

Work in garter stitch for ½" (13mm).

Bind off loosely.

SLEEVES *(make 2)*

Place 44 (48, 50, 52, 54, 55) sleeve stitches onto larger needles.

Cast on 2 (2, 2, 3, 3, 4) stitches, knit the sleeve stitches, cast on 2 (2, 2, 3, 3, 4) stitches. Place a marker and join for working in the round—48 (52, 54, 58, 60, 63) stitches.

Knit 1 round.

Decrease round: Ssk, knit to the last 2 stitches, k2tog.

Continue in stockinette stitch, work Decrease round every 8 (8, 7, 8, 8, 9) rounds 4 (6, 1, 3, 4, 6) times and then every 9 (9, 8, 9, 9, 10) rounds 2 (1, 7, 5, 5, 3) times, ending with a right-side row—34 (36, 36, 40, 40, 43) stitches remain.

Ruffled Cuff

Note: Work flat on the smaller needle with the yarn for the cuff. The ruffle yarn may cause your stitches to be larger than usual.

Change to smaller needle and holding MC and CC together, work back and forth in garter stitch.

Increase row (WS): K1, kfb, knit to the last 2 stitches, kfb, k1 (2 stitches increased for seam).

Work even in garter stitch until cuff measures 3½ (4, 4½, 4¾, 5¼, 5¾)" (9 [10, 11.5, 12, 13, 14.5]cm), or desired length.

Bind off loosely with MC only.

FRONT AND NECK EDGING

With the right side facing and using MC and smaller needles, start at the lower front corner and pick up and knit 49 (51, 54, 59, 63, 70) stitches along the right front edge, pick up and knit 8 (8, 8, 8, 8, 7) stitches across the top of the sleeve, pick up and knit 17 (15, 17, 18, 20, 23) stitches across the back neck, pick up and knit 8 (8, 8, 8, 8, 7) stitches across the top of the second sleeve, then pick up and knit 49 (51, 54, 59, 63, 70) stitches along the left front edge—131 (133, 141, 152, 162, 200) stitches.

Knit 5 rows.

Bind off loosely.

I-CORD TIE (*make 2*)

With MC and smaller needle, cast on 7 stitches.

Row 1: K4; with yarn in front, slip the last 3 stitches purlwise.

Row 2: Give yarn a slight tug, k4; with yarn in front, slip the last 3 stitches purlwise.

Repeat row 2 until the tie measures 21 (22, 23, 25, 27, 29)" (53.5 [56, 58.5, 63.5, 68.5, 74]cm). This creates a tie with I-cord edges and a single garter stitch in the center.

Bind off 3 stitches; with yarn in front, slip the last 3 stitches purlwise.

Bind off 3 stitches; cut yarn and pull through the last stitch.

FINISHING

Weave in the ends. Sew a tie to each front corner for closure.

tip: Keep a piece of scrap paper handy to record your raglan increases and front neckline increases as you knit. These increases grow at different rates to accommodate the complex shaping required!

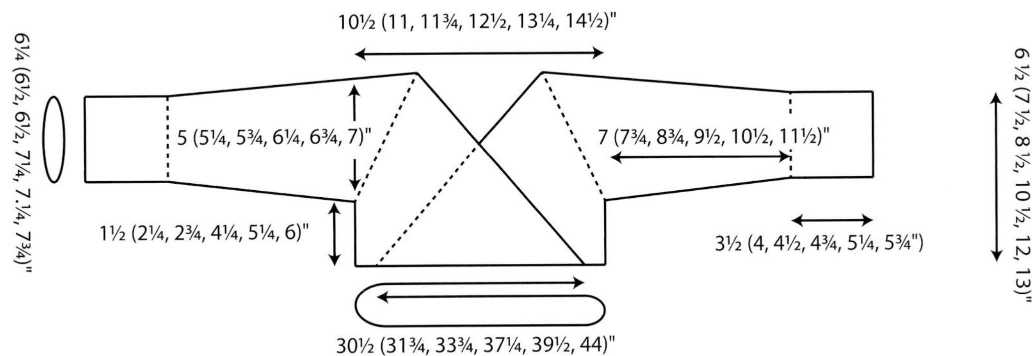

satya doll ballet wrap

skill level

Advanced

finished measurement

Chest circumference: 11-13" (28-33cm)

materials

- Sublime Baby Silk & Bamboo DK, 80% bamboo-sourced viscose, 20% silk, 1¾ oz (50g), 105 yd (96m); 1 ball in #270 (MC) (3)
- Filatura Di Crosa Bandel, 75% cotton, 25% polyamide, 1¾ oz (50g), 77 yd (70m); 1 skein in #7 Opal (CC)
- Size U.S. 6 (4mm) circular needle, 24" (61cm) length, or size needed to obtain gauge
- Size U.S. 5 (3.75mm) double-pointed needles
- 4 stitch markers
- 2 stitch holders
- Darning needle

gauge

5½ stitches and 7½ rows = 1" (2.5cm) in stockinette stitch on larger needle

YOKE

With the larger needle and MC, cast on 2 front stitches, place a marker, cast on 5 sleeve stitches, place a marker, cast on 16 back stitches, place a marker, cast on 5 sleeve stitches, place a marker, cast on 2 front stitches–30 stitches.

Increase row (RS): Knit into the front and back of the stitch (kfb), *knit to 1 stitch before the marker, kfb, slip the marker, kfb; repeat from * 3 times more, knit to the last stitch, kfb (10 stitches increased).

Next row: Purl.

Repeat the last 2 rows 9 times more (10 increase rounds total)–130 stitches.

divide sleeves from body

Next row (RS): Kfb, k21, cast on 6 stitches, place 25 sleeve stitches on holder, k36, cast on 6 stitches, place 25 sleeve stitches on holder, k21, kfb–144 stitches.

Next row: Purl.

Increase row: Kfb, knit to the last stitch, kfb.

Repeat the last 2 rows 6 times more–158 stitches.

Knit 3 rows.

Bind off loosely.

SLEEVES (*make 2*)

Place 25 sleeve stitches onto larger needles.

Cast on 3 stitches, knit sleeve stitches, cast on 3 stitches–31 stitches. Place a marker and join for working in the round.

Work in stockinette stitch for 1½" (3.8cm).

ruffled cuff

Change to smaller needle and holding MC and CC together, work back and forth in garter stitch.

Increase row (WS): K1, kfb, knit to the last 2 stitches, kfb, k1 (2 stitches increased for seam).

Work even in garter stitch until cuff measures 1¼" (3cm) or until sleeve measures desired length.

Bind off loosely with MC only.

I-CORD TIES (*make 2*)

With MC, cast on 7 stitches.

Row 1: K4; with yarn in front, slip the last 3 stitches purlwise.

Row 2: Give the yarn a slight tug, k4; with yarn in front, slip the last 3 stitches purlwise.

Repeat row 2 until the tie measures 12" (30.5cm). This creates a tie with I-cord edges and a single garter stitch in the center.

Bind off 3 stitches; with yarn in front, slip the last 3 stitches purlwise.

Bind off 3 stitches; cut yarn and pull through the last stitch.

FINISHING

Weave in the ends. Sew a tie to each front corner for closure.

---

tip: You may choose to work front and neck edging to match the child's version (page 69) by picking up all around and working a few rows in garter stitch; however, it is not necessary because of this project's small size.

kaylee beaded skirt

Most little girls I know love sequins and sparkles, so to make this summery hemp and cotton-blend skirt extra special, I added shiny beads at the edging. The yarn has a texture and drape to it that cannot be matched by many fibers. If you've never worked with beads, you'll be amazed at how quick and easy it is to knit them into the fabric using just a steel crochet hook.

skill level

Intermediate

sizes

4 (6, 8, 10, 12) years. Shown in size 8.

finished measurements

Hip circumference: 24 (24, 27, 30, 33)" (61 [61, 68.5, 76, 84]cm)

Length: 11 (14, 15, 16, 17½)" (28 [35.5, 38, 40.5, 44.5] cm)

materials

- Elsebeth Lavold Hempathy, 41% cotton, 34% hemp, 25% modal, 1¾ oz (50g) 154 yd (140m); 2 (3, 3, 3, 4) balls in #8 Turquoise (2)
- Size U.S. 4 (3.5mm) circular needle, 24" (61cm) length, or size to obtain gauge
- Size U.S. 3 (3.25mm) circular needle, 24" (61cm) length
- Size 11, 12, or 13 (.80, .75, .70mm) steel crochet hook
- 5 stitch markers (1 of color A and 4 of color B)
- Darning needle
- 144 (144, 162, 180, 198) size 6/0 beads, plus extra in case of breakage

gauge

6 stitches and 8½ rows = 1" (2.5cm) in stockinette stitch

notes

Refer to Special Stitches and Techniques (page 151) for instructions on the k1, p1 ribs and backward-loop cast-on.

Refer to Knitting with Beads (page 78), for complete instructions on how to add beads as you knit.

SKIRT

With smaller needle, cast on 124 (132, 142, 152, 162) stitches. Place a marker A and join for working in the round (marker indicates center back).

Work in k1, p1 rib for 2" (5cm).

Change to larger needle and work 4 rounds even in stockinette stitch.

hip shaping

Note: Create m1 hip increases using a backward-loop cast-on *or* by picking up the bar between the stitches to be knit and then knitting into the back loop to twist the stitch (for a cleaner increase).

Round 1: *K15 (17, 18, 19, 20), m1, place a marker B, k32 (32, 35, 38, 41), place a marker B, m1, k15 (17, 18, 19, 20); repeat from * once more–128 (136, 146, 156, 166) stitches.

Rounds 2-4: Work even in stockinette stitch.

Round 5: *Knit to marker B, m1, slip the marker, knit to the next marker B, slip the marker, m1; repeat from * once more–132 (140, 150, 160, 170) stitches.

Repeat rounds 2-5, 3 (1, 3, 5, 7) times more–144 (144, 162, 180, 198) stitches.

Work even in stockinette stitch until skirt measures 9½ (12½, 13½, 14½, 16)" (24 [32, 34.5, 37, 40.5]cm) from the cast-on edge.

LACE EDGING (*multiple of 18 stitches*)

Round 1: *K3 [add a bead, k1] 6 times, k3; repeat from * to the end.

Round 2: Purl.

Round 3: *[K2tog] 3 times, [yarn over, k1] 6 times, [k2tog] 3 times; repeat from * to the end.

Round 4: Knit.

Repeat rounds 1-4 twice more.

Bind off loosely.

FINISHING

Weave in the ends.

Block, if desired, taking extra care to pin down each curve of the lace edging repeat to a blocking board. Do not stretch the skirt beyond the finished hip circumference measurement.

---

tip: I designed this skirt with zero ease so that it's easy to determine which size to knit. But if you find that the skirt slips off your recipient too easily, make a simple tie closure by braiding 3 strands of yarn and then threading the braid through the top ribbing.

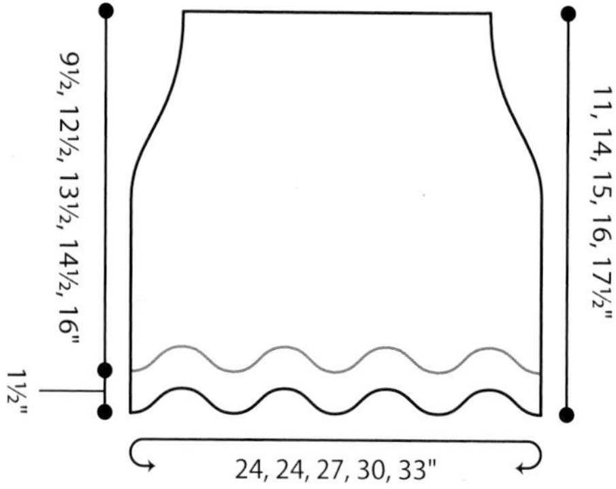

KNITTING WITH BEADS

Using a steel crochet hook to add beads into your knitting is a deceptively easy method. You need spend no time prestringing your beads, and it takes one quick little motion to slip the bead onto your stitch with the crochet hook. When using this method the bead will sit on the actual stitch rather than between the stitches, which happens when using other methods.

When you come to a stitch to bead, follow these steps:

Step 1: Slip 1 bead onto the crochet hook.

Step 2: Insert the hook into the stitch you are about to knit. Pull the stitch off the knitting needle so it is resting in the crook of the crochet hook. You may now slip the bead down off the crochet hook to rest on the stitch.

Step 3: Slip the knit stitch back onto your left needle.

Step 4: Knit or slip the stitch just beaded.

That's it! This method is so easy, you'll want to add beads to everything you knit.

kaylee doll beaded skirt

skill level

Intermediate

finished measurement

Waist circumference:
12" (30.5cm)

materials

- Elsebeth Lavold Hempathy, 41% cotton, 34% hemp, 25% modal, 1¾ oz (50g), 154 yd (140m), 1 ball in #8 Turquoise (2)
- Size U.S. 4 (3.5mm) double-pointed needles, or circular needle for Magic Loop method, or size to obtain gauge
- Size U.S. 3 (3.25mm) double-pointed needles, or circular needle for Magic Loop method
- Size 11, 12, or 13 (.80, .75, .70mm) steel crochet hook
- 2 stitch markers
- Darning needle
- 72 size 6/0 beads, plus extra in case of breakage

gauge

6 stitches and 8½ rows = 1" (2.5cm) in stockinette stich

notes

Refer to Special Stitches and Techniques (page 151) for instructions on the k1, p1 rib, and Magic Loop method.

Refer to Knitting with Beads, page 78, for complete instructions on how to add beads as you knit.

SKIRT

With the smaller needle, cast on 60 stitches. Place a marker and join for working in the round.

Work in k1, p1 rib for 1½" (3.8cm).

Change to the larger needle. K30, place a marker, and knit to the end. Work 3 rounds even in stockinette stitch.

hip shaping

Note: Create m1 hip increases using a backward-loop cast on *or* by picking up the bar between the stitches to be knit and then knitting into the back loop to twist the stitch (for a cleaner increase).

Round 1: *K7, m1, k16, m1, k7; repeat from * once more—64 stitches.

Rounds 2-4: Knit.

Round 5: *K7, m1, k18, m1, k7; repeat from * once more—68 stitches.

Rounds 6-8: Knit.

Round 9: *K7, m1, k20, m1, k7; repeat from * once more—72 stitches.

Work even in stockinette stitch until skirt measures 3½" (9cm) from the cast-on edge.

LACE EDGING *(multiple of 18 stitches)*

Round 1: *K3 [add a bead, k1] 6 times, k3; repeat from * around.

Round 2: Purl.

Round 3: *[K2tog] 3 times, [yarn over, k1] 6 times, [k2tog] 3 times; repeat from * around.

Round 4: Knit.

Repeat rounds 1-4 twice more.

Bind off loosely.

FINISHING

Weave in the ends. Block and make tie closure, if desired (Tip, page 77), as for child's skirt.

elliot cabled vest

This little vest dresses up casual outfits and can be worn to almost any special occasion—perfect for spring pictures or the first day of school. An astonishingly easy-to-memorize stitch repeat creates a cable pattern that looks complicated to knit but instead flows with ease.

materials

- Spud & Chloë Sweater, 55% superwash wool, 45% organic cotton, 3½ oz (100g), 160 yd (146m); 2 (2, 2, 3, 3, 3) skeins in #7524 Chocolate Milk (4)
- Size U.S. 8 (5mm) circular needle, 16" (40.5cm) length
- Size U.S. 8 (5mm) double-pointed needles for sleeves, or size to obtain gauge
- Size U.S. 7 (4.5mm) circular needle, 16" (40.5cm) length, 1 size smaller than gauge, and double-pointed needles for sleeves
- 1 stitch marker
- Cable needle
- 3 stitch holders
- Darning needle

gauge

4½ stitches and 6¼ rows = 1" (2.5cm) in Wave Cable pattern

note

Refer to Special Stitches and Techniques (page 151) for instructions on the k1, p1 rib, and three-needle bind-off.

If you like reading charts, use the Wave Cable Chart on page 85, where that stitch pattern is indicated in the instructions.

skill level
Advanced

sizes
2 (4, 6, 8, 10) years.
Shown in size 2.

finished measurements
Chest circumference:
23¼ (24¾, 26½, 28, 29½, 31)" (59 [63, 67.5, 71, 75.5, 79]cm)
Length: 13 (14, 15, 17, 18, 18¾)" (33 [35.5, 38, 43, 45.5, 47.5]cm)

BODY

With the smaller needle, cast on 95 (100, 106, 112, 122, 130) stitches. Place a marker and join for working in the round.

Work in k1, p1 rib for 1½" (3.8cm).

Change to the larger needle.

Increase round: *K8 (7, 7, 10, 12), knit through the front and back of the next stitch (kfb); repeat from *9 (11, 12, 13, 10, 9) times more, k5 (4, 2, 0, 1, 0)–105 (112, 119, 126, 133, 140) stitches.

Work the Wave Cable pattern as follows:

Rounds 1-2: Knit.

Round 3: *[Slip 2 stitches onto the cable needle and hold to the back of the work; knit next 2 stitches; knit 2 stitches from the cable needle (2/2 RC)], k3; repeat from * around.

Rounds 4-6: Knit.

Round 7: *K2, 2/2 RC, k1; repeat from * around.

Rounds 8-10: Knit.

Round 11: Repeat round 3.

Round 12: Knit.

Repeat rounds 1-12 until the piece measures 7 (8, 9, 10, 10½, 11)" (18 [20.5, 23, 25.5, 26.5, 28] cm) from the cast-on edge, ending on an even-numbered round. Divide for front and back as follows:

Next round (RS): Work 0 (0, 1, 0, 5, 0) stitches, bind off 4 stitches, work 48 (52, 55, 59, 62, 66) stitches in pattern, place remaining 53 (56, 60, 63, 67, 70) back stitches on a holder. This row helps center the cable on the front.

FRONT

Note: As you work you will continue in the Wave Cable pattern as established. If there are not enough stitches on the ends to work the cable as you decrease for neck and armhole, work those side stitches in stockinette stitch as needed.

Next row (WS): Bind off 4 stitches, purl to the end–44 (48, 52, 55, 58, 62) stitches remain.

Decrease row (RS): K1, ssk, work in pattern to last 3 stitches, k2tog, k1–42 (46, 50, 53, 56, 60) stitches remain.

Continuing in pattern as established, repeat decrease row every right-side row, 0 (0, 1, 2, 3, 4) times more–46 (48, 49, 50, 52) stitches remain.

Work even in pattern until piece measures 10 (11, 12, 14, 15, 15¾)" (25 [28, 30.5, 35.5, 38, 40] cm) from cast-on edge, ending with a wrong-side row.

neck shaping

Next row: Work 16 (18, 19, 19, 19, 20) stitches, bind off center 10 (10, 10, 11, 12, 12) stitches, work to end.

right front

Rows 1 and 3 (WS): Work in pattern to end.
Rows 2 and 4: Bind off 2 stitches, work to end–12 (14, 15, 15, 15, 16) stitches after row 4.
Rows 5, 7, 9, and 11: Work in pattern to end.
Rows 6, 8, 10, and 12 (RS): K1, ssk, work to end–8 (10, 11, 11, 11, 12) stitches after row 12.
Continue in pattern as established until piece measures 13 (14, 15, 17, 18, 18¾)" (33 [35.5, 38, 43, 45.5, 47.5]cm) from the cast-on edge.
Place stitches onto a holder.

left front

Rows 1 and 3 (WS): Bind off 2 stitches, work to end–12 (14, 15, 15, 15, 16) stitches after row 3.
Rows 2 and 4: Work in pattern to end.
Rows 5, 7, 9, and 11: Work in pattern to end.
Rows 6, 8, 10, and 12: Work to the last 3 stitches, k2tog, k1–8 (10, 11, 11, 11, 12) stitches after row 12.
Continue in pattern as established until piece measures 13 (14, 15, 17, 18, 18¾)" (33 [35.5, 38, 43, 45.5, 47.5]cm) from the cast-on edge.
Place stitches onto a holder.

BACK

Note: As you work you will continue in the Wave Cable pattern as established. If there are not enough stitches on the ends to work the cable as you make the decreases, work those side stitches in stockinette stitch as needed.
Place back stitches onto larger needles ready to work a right-side row. Continuing in the Wave Cable pattern as established, bind off 4 stitches at the beginning of the next 2 rows–45 (48, 52, 55, 59, 62) stitches.
Decrease row (RS): K1, ssk, work to the last 3 stitches, k2tog, k1–43 (46, 50, 53, 57, 60) stitches remain.
Continuing in pattern as established, repeat decrease row every right-side row 0 (0, 1, 2, 3, 4) times more–43 (46, 48, 49, 51, 52) stitches remain.
Continue in pattern as established until back measures 13 (14, 15, 17, 18, 18¾)" (33 [35.5, 38, 43, 45.5, 47.5]cm) from the cast-on edge.
Next row: Work 8 (10, 11, 11, 11, 12) stitches, bind off the next 27 (26, 26, 27, 29, 28) stitches, knit to the end.
Place the front shoulder stitches onto needles.
Join front and back shoulders using the three-needle bind-off, or graft stitches together.

ARMBAND *(make 2)*

With the right side facing and starting at the center of the underarm, use the smaller needle to pick up and knit 56 (56, 60, 66, 70, 72) stitches evenly around the armhole.
Work 5 rounds in k1, p1 rib.
Bind off in pattern.

NECK BAND

With the right side facing and starting at the right shoulder seam, use the smaller needle to pick up and knit 70 (70, 70, 72, 74, 74) stitches evenly around the neck opening.
Work 5 rounds in k1, p1 rib.
Bind off in pattern.

FINISHING

Weave in the ends. Block, if desired.

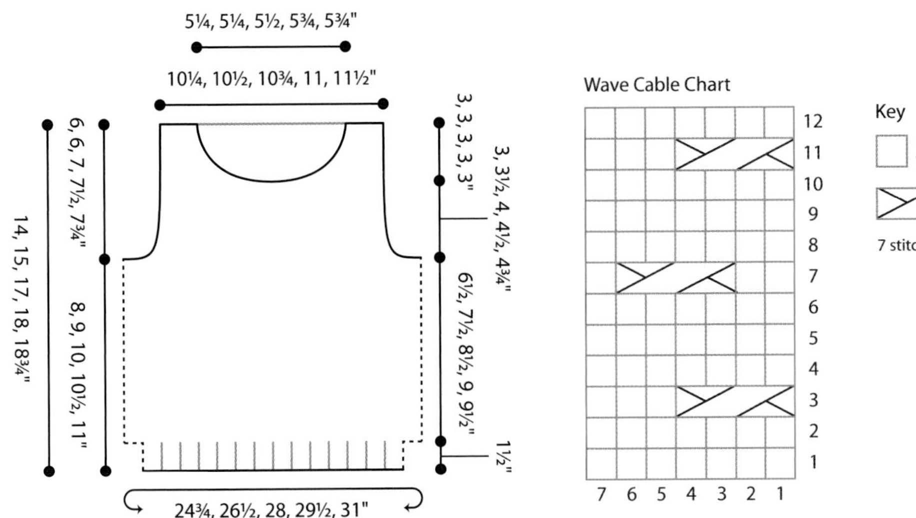
5¼, 5¼, 5½, 5¾, 5¾"
10¼, 10½, 10¾, 11, 11½"
14, 15, 17, 18, 18¾"
6, 6, 7, 7½, 7¾"
8, 9, 10, 10½, 11"
3, 3, 3, 3, 3"
3, 3½, 4, 4½, 4¾"
6½, 7½, 8½, 9, 9½"
1½"
24¾, 26½, 28, 29½, 31"
Wave Cable Chart
12
11
10
9
8
7
6
5
4
3
2
1
7 6 5 4 3 2 1
Key
RS: Knit
WS: Purl
2/2 RC
7 stitch Pattern Repeat

elliot doll cabled vest

skill level
Advanced

finished measurement
Chest circumference: 11–13" (28–33cm)

materials

- Spud & Chloë Sweater, 55% superwash wool, 45% organic cotton, 3½ oz (100g), 160 yd (146m); 1 skein in #7524 Chocolate Milk (4)
- Size U.S. 8 (5mm) double-pointed needles, or circular needle for Magic Loop method, or size to obtain gauge
- Size U.S. 7 (4.5mm) double-pointed needles, or circular needle for Magic Loop method
- 3 stitch markers
- Stitch holder
- 2 buttons, ½" (13mm)
- Darning needle
- Cable needle

gauge

4½ stitches and 6¼ rows = 1" (2.5cm) in Wave Cable pattern

notes

Refer to Special Stitches and Techniques (page 151) for instructions on the k1, p1 rib.

BODY

With the smaller needle, cast on 62 stitches. Place a marker and join for working in the round.

Work 3 rounds in k1, p1 rib.

Change to larger needle.

Next round: K12, place a marker, work 7 stitches of the Wave Cable pattern (page 83; or refer to the chart on page 85), place a marker, k12, place a marker (side seam), knit to the end.

Work in pattern as established until sweater measures 3½" (9cm) from the cast-on edge.

Dividing round: Bind off 5 stitches, k26, and place the remaining 31 back stitches onto a holder.

FRONT

Next row (WS): Bind off 5 stitches, work in pattern to end.

Continue in pattern as established for 1½" (3.8cm), ending on a wrong-side row.

Next row (RS): K5, bind off 11 stitches, knit to the end.

right front

Continue in stockinette stitch on last 5 stitches for 1¾" (4.5cm). Bind off loosely.

left front

Work same as for right front.

BACK

Place back stitches onto larger needles ready to work a right-side row. Working in stockinette stitch, bind off 5 stitches at the beginning of the next 2 rows—21 stitches.

Next row (RS): K9, bind off 3 stitches, knit to the end.

Work in stockinette stitch on 9 stitches for 3¼" (8cm) separately for each back. Bind off loosely.

SHOULDER SEAMS

Starting from the armhole edge, sew front 5 stitches to 5 stitches of back. Repeat for other side.

ARMBANDS (*make 2*)

With the right side facing and smaller needle, starting at the center of the underarm, pick up and knit 32 stitches evenly around the armhole. Work 3 rounds in k1, p1 rib. Bind off in pattern.

NECK BAND

With the right side facing and smaller needle, starting at the left back center, pick up and knit 34 stitches evenly around the neck opening, ending at the right back center. Work 3 rows in k1, p1 rib. Bind off in pattern.

RIGHT BACK PLACKET

With the right side facing and smaller needle, starting at the lower left edge of the neck band, pick up and knit 18 stitches evenly along back opening and neck band.

Row 1 (WS): *K1, p1; repeat from * to end.

Row 2: *[K1, p1] twice, ssk, yarn over; repeat from * once more, [k1, p1] 3 times.

Row 3: Repeat row 1.

Bind off in pattern.

LEFT BACK PLACKET

With the right side facing and smaller needle, starting at the lower left edge of the back opening, pick up and knit 18 stitches evenly along the back opening and edge of neck band.
Work 3 rounds in k1, p1 rib.
Bind off in pattern.

FINISHING

Place the Right Placket over the Left Placket and sew the bottom edges to the lower edge of the center back opening. Sew the buttons onto the left back placket opposite the buttonholes on the right placket. Weave in the ends.

nicole lace shrug

For this lovely shrug, I hearkened back to a bygone era, imagining what Elizabeth Bennet, my favorite of Jane Austen's heroines, might have worn as a child. Complex open stitchwork at the back of the shrug gives it an elegant and classic look, while the shawl collar provides a little warmth for cool summer nights and chilly fall days.

materials

- SweetGeorgia Superwash Worsted, 100% superwash merino wool, 4 oz (114g) 200 yd (182.9m); 1 (2, 2, 2, 2) skeins in Savory (4)
- Size U.S. 7 (4.5mm) circular needle, 24" (61cm) length, for sizes 4 and 6
- Size U.S. 8 (5mm) circular needle, 24" (61cm) length, for sizes 8 and 10
- Size U.S. 9 (5.5mm) circular needle, 24" (61cm) length, for size 12
- Stitch marker
- Darning needle

gauge

4½ stitches = 1" (2.5cm) in Diamond Lace pattern for sizes 4 and 6

4¼ stitches = 1" (2.5cm) in Diamond Lace pattern for sizes 8 and 10

4 stitches = 1" (2.5cm) in Diamond Lace pattern for size 12

note

Refer to Special Stitches and Techniques (page 151) for instructions on the backward-loop cast-on.

skill level

Intermediate

sizes

4 (6, 8, 10, 12) years. Shown in size 6.

finished measurements

Across back: 9½ (10, 10½, 11, 11½)" (24 [25.5, 26.5, 28, 29.5]cm)

BODY

Note: Create m1 increases by picking up the bar between the stitches to be knit and then knitting into the back loop.

Cast on 48 stitches.

Next row (RS) K2, *p2, k2; repeat from * to end.

Work in k2, p2 rib as established for 1¾" (4.5cm).

Setup row (RS): K1, *k4, yarn over, ssk, k3, k2tog, yarn over, k5; repeat from * to the last 15 stitches, k4, yarn over, ssk, k3, k2tog, yarn over, k3, m1, k1—49 stitches.

Next row: Purl.

Next row (RS): Beginning with row 4 of the chart, work the Diamond Lace pattern; repeat to row 16.

separate sleeves from back

Next row (WS): Bind off 24 stitches, purl to the end.

BACK

Beginning with row 2 of the chart, continue in the Diamond Lace pattern as established, working a [slip, slip, knit (ssk)] instead of a [slip 1, k2tog, pass slipped stitch over (sk2p)] at the end of each row 6 until the back measures 9½ (10, 10½, 11, 11½)" (24 [25.5, 26.5, 28, 29.5]cm) from the bind-off edge , ending with a right-side row.

Cast on 24 stitches at the end of this row using the backward-loop cast-on—49 stitches.

Next row (WS): Purl.

Continuing in Diamond Lace pattern, work 15 more rows, decreasing 1 stitch at the beginning of the last row (RS)—48 stitches.

Next row (WS): P2, *k2, p2; repeat from * to end.

Work in k2, p2 rib as established for 1¾" (4.5cm).

Bind off loosely in rib.

Sew sleeve seams.

EDGING

With right side facing and starting at the left underarm seam, pick up and knit 44 (48, 48, 50, 46) stitches across the lower back edge, 16 (16, 16, 16, 12) stitches along the right front edge, 44 (48, 48, 50, 46) stitches across the upper back edge, and 16 (16, 16, 16, 12) stitches along the left front edge—120 (128, 128, 132, 116) stitches. Place a marker and join for working in the round.

Work in k2, p2 rib for 2" (5cm).

Bind off loosely in rib.

FINISHING

Weave in the ends. Block, if desired.

Diamond Lace Pattern

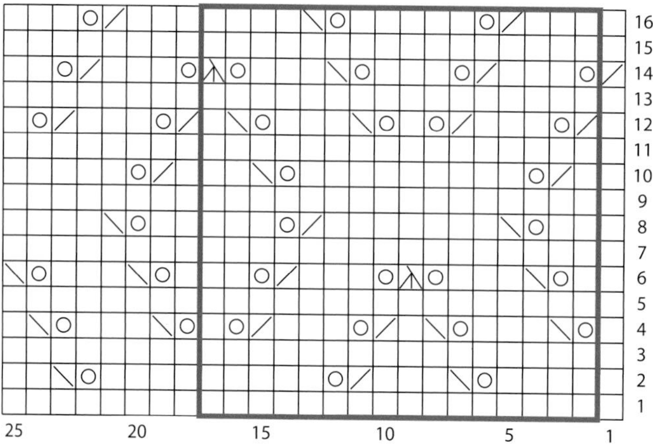

Key

RS: Knit
WS: Purl

yo

ssk

k2tog

sk2p

indicates pattern stitch repeat

NOTE: Do not work centered double decreases as the first or last stitch of a row; instead, work a k2tog or ssk. Always be sure that you work one yarn over for each stitch decreased.

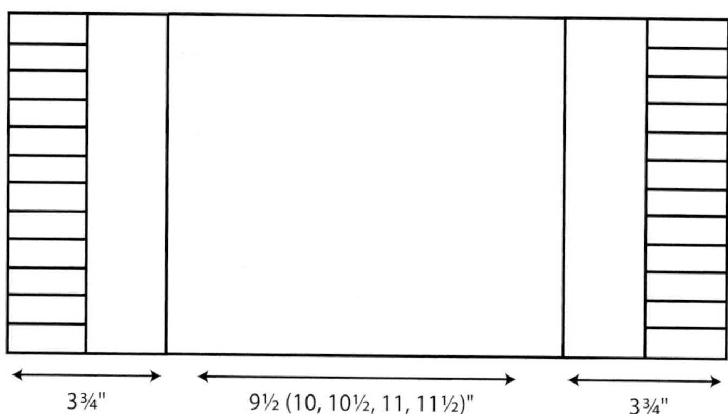

nicole doll lace shrug

skill level

Intermediate

finished measurement

Across back: 5" (12.5cm)

materials

- SweetGeorgia Superwash Worsted, 100% superwash merino wool, 4 oz (114g) 200 yd (182.9m); 1 skein in Saffron (4)
- Size U.S. 7 (4.5mm) circular needle, 16" (40.5cm) length
- 3 stitch markers (1 of color A and 2 of color B)
- Darning needle

gauge

4¾ stitches and 7 rows = 1" (2.5cm) in Diamond Lace pattern

note

Refer to Special Stitches and Techniques (page 151) for instructions on the backward-loop cast-on.

RIGHT SLEEVE

Cast on 34 stitches.

Next row (RS): K2, *p2, k2; repeat from * to end.

Work in k2, p2 rib as established for 2" (5cm).

BODY

Next row (RS): Bind off 17 stitches, then work row 2 of the Diamond Lace pattern chart (page 93).

Continue the Diamond Lace pattern until the chart has been completed, working a [slip, slip, knit (ssk)] instead of a [slip 1, k2tog, pass slipped stitch over (sk2p)] at the end of row 14.

LEFT SLEEVE

Next row (WS): Purl to end, cast on 17 stitches using the backward-loop cast-on.

Next row: K2, *p2, k2; repeat from * to end.

Work in k2, p2 rib as established for 2" (5cm). Bind off in pattern.

Sew ribbed sleeve seams. This seam marks the bottom of the sleeves.

SHAWL COLLAR

With right side facing and starting at the left underarm seam, pick up and knit 20 stitches across the bottom edge of the back, 16 stitches across the right sleeve edge, placing a marker B at center of these 16 stitches, 20 stitches across the top edge of the back, and 16 stitches across the left sleeve edge, placing a marker B at the center of these 16 stitches—72 stitches.

Place a marker A and join for knitting in the round.

Work 8 rounds in k2, p2 rib.

short rows

Row 1 (RS): Continue in rib pattern, work to 1 stitch before the second B marker, bring the working yarn to the front and slip the next stitch from the left needle to the right needle (this is the first step in wrapping this stitch). Turn your work and remove the marker.

Row 2: Slip the first (unworked) stitch from the left needle to the right needle and work the next stitch (this is the second step in wrapping this stitch). Continue to work until 1 stitch before the first B marker, wrap and turn. Remove the marker.

Row 3: Work to 1 stitch before the last wrapped stitch, wrap and turn.

Repeat the last row 5 times more—4 wrapped stitches each side.

Continue to the end of round, lifting the wraps and working them together with the wrapped stitch.

Next round: Work in k2, p2 rib as established to the first wrapped stitch. Insert the needle through the wrap, which appears as a horizontal bar at the base of the wrapped stitch, and then through the wrapped stitch, and knit or purl both stitches together.

Continue to the end of the round, picking up the wrapped stitches as you go.

Bind off loosely in rib.

FINISHING

Weave in the ends.

michelle mermaid bracelets

Every evening my oldest daughter plays lovingly with her mermaid dolls in the bathtub, so I dreamed up this matching mermaid jewelry and doll costume for fish-out-of-water fun. Make a bracelet for both doll and child to wear; the tiny mermaid doll tail, page 100, completes the play set.

materials

- Elsebeth Lavold Hempathy, 41% cotton, 34% hemp, 25% modal, 1¾ oz (50g), 154 yd (140m); 1 ball each in #47 Emerald Green and #49 Mustard (2)
- Size U.S. 4 (3.5mm) needle, or size to obtain gauge
- Safety pin
- Size 14 (.75mm) steel crochet hook
- Approximately 126 (138) size 6/0 beads, plus extra in case of breakage
- Toggle clasp
- Darning needle

gauge

Approximately 14 rows = 1" (2.5cm) in pattern

note

Refer to Knitting with Beads (page 78), for complete instructions on how to add beads as you knit.

skill level
Intermediate

sizes
Small (Medium).
Shown in Small.

finished measurements
Length: 6¼ (6¾)" (15.5 [17]cm) without clasp
Width: ½" (13mm)

BRACELETS (*make 3*)

Cast on 7 stitches.

Row 1 (RS): K4; with yarn in front, slip the last 3 stitches purlwise.

Row 2: Give the yarn a slight tug, k4; with yarn in front, slip the last 3 stitches purlwise.

Row 3: Give the yarn a slight tug, k3, add a bead; with yarn in front, slip the last 3 stitches purlwise.

Note: Place the safety pin on the right side of the work to mark which side to work beads.

Repeat rows 2 and 3 until bracelet measures 6¼ (6¾)" (15.5 [17]cm) or desired length, ending with row 2.

Next row: Bind off 3 stitches; with yarn in front, slip the last 3 stitches purlwise.

Bind off 3 stitches; cut the yarn and pull it through the last stitch.

FINISHING

Weave in the ends. Block if desired.

Sew the toggle clasp securely to each end of the bracelet.

RUB-A-DUB BABY

It would not seem right for me to write a book about children and dolls without telling this particular story that I grew up hearing from my mother—a black-haired, olive skinned beauty. In the late seventies there was a commercial for a particular doll called Rub-A-Dub Dolly. One variation of the doll had curly blond hair and blue eyes, and when my mother was pregnant with me, she told everyone I was going to look like that doll. It isn't hard to imagine that most people thought this prediction was just the pregnancy hormones talking (and I am sure it was), but when I was born I came out with all my father's Irish genes screaming: pale skin, big blue eyes, and curly blond hair. And my mom proudly told everyone she had given birth to Rub-A-Dub Dolly!

michelle doll mermaid tail

skill level
Intermediate

finished measurement
Waist circumference:
12" (30.5cm)

materials

- Elsebeth Lavold Hempathy, 41% cotton, 34% hemp, 25% modal, 1¾ oz (50g), 154 yd (140m); 1 ball in #47 Emerald Green (2)
- Size U.S. 4 (3.5mm) double-pointed needles or circular needle for Magic Loop method, or size to obtain gauge
- Size U.S. 3 (3.25mm) double-pointed needles or circular needle for Magic Loop method
- Stitch marker
- Darning needle

gauge

6 stitches and 8 rows = 1" (2.5cm) in Scale Stitch on larger needles

notes

Refer to Special Stitches and Techniques (page 151) for instructions on the backward-loop cast-on and Magic Loop method.

BODY

With smaller needles, cast on 72 stitches. Place a marker and join for working in the round.

Work a k1, p1 rib until pieces measure 1½" (3.8cm) from the cast-on edge.

Change to larger needles and work the Scale Stitch pattern as follows:

Round 1: *Knit into the front and back of the stitch (kfb), [slip 1 stitch, k1, pass slipped stitch over (skp)], k5; repeat from * to the end.

Round 2 and all even-numbered rounds: Knit.

Round 3: *Kfb, k1, skp, k4; repeat from * to the end.

Round 5: *Kfb, k2, skp, k3: repeat from * to the end.

Round 7: *Kfb, k3, skp, k2; repeat from * to the end.

Round 9: *Kfb, k4, skp, k1; repeat from * to the end.

Round 11: *Kfb, k5, skp; repeat from * to the end.

Round 12: Knit.

Repeat rounds 1–12 of the Scale Stitch pattern until the tail measures 8" (20.5cm) or desired length.

decrease for tail

Next round: *K4, k2tog; repeat from * around—60 stitches.

Divide the stitches evenly onto working needles. We are going to knit the front and back stitches together to close the bottom but continue with stitches on the needle for the tail.

With the smaller needle in the right hand and the working needles together in the left hand (one in front of the other), *knit the first stitch on the front needle together with the first stitch on the back needle; repeat from * to end—30 stitches.

TAIL

Rows 1 and 3 (WS): *K2, p2; repeat from * to the last 2 stitches, k2.

Row 2: *P2, k2; repeat from * to the last 2 stitches, p2.

Row 4: P2, m1 using the backward-loop cast-on, k2, *p2, m1, k2; repeat from * to the last 2 stitches, p2—37 stitches.

Row 5: K2, *p3, k2; repeat from * to end.

Row 6: P2, *k3, p2; repeat from * to end.

Repeat rows 5 and 6 until the ribbed section of the tail measures 1½" (3.8cm).

Increase row (WS): *K2, increase 1, p3; repeat from * to the last 2 stitches, k2—44 stitches.

Next row: P2, *k3, p3; repeat from * to end.

Continue in rib as established until ribbed section of tail measures 4" (10cm).

Bind off loosely in pattern.

FINISHING

Block the tail so that the scales sit flat and look their best. Be careful not to stretch the tail out so that it isn't too loose on the doll.

---

tip: If you find the tail slips off the doll too easily, make a simple tie closure by braiding 3 strands of yarn and then threading the braid through the top ribbing.

---

laura camisole

Since moving to Georgia I've lived through many hot summers, and my go-to warm weather knits are tops like this camisole—dressy enough to look pulled-together, but breathable enough to provide relief from the heat. I've chosen a bamboo-and-silk yarn that will be smooth and cool against a child's sensitive skin and lend lovely stitch definition to this lattice design.

skill level
Intermediate

sizes
2 (4, 6, 8, 10) years. Shown in size 4.

finished measurements
Chest circumference: 22 (23½, 25, 25¾, 28)" (56 [59.5, 63.5, 65.5, 71]cm)
Length: 10½ (11, 11½, 13, 14)" (26.5 [28, 29.5, 33, 35.5]cm) without straps

materials

- Sublime Baby Silk & Bamboo DK, 80% bamboo-sourced viscose, 20% silk; 1¾ oz (50g), 104 yd (95m); 3 (4, 5, 6, 7) balls in #269 Light Blue (2)
- Size U.S. 5 (3.75mm) circular needle, 16" (40.5cm) length, or size to obtain gauge
- Size U.S. 3 (3.25mm) circular needle, 16" (40.5cm) length
- 4 stitch markers (2 of color A and 2 of color B)
- 3 stitch holders
- Darning needle

gauge

5 stitches and 7 rows = 1" (2.5cm) in stockinette stitch

special stitches

1/1 RC (Right Cross)
Knit the second stitch on the left needle, passing in *front* of the first stitch. Knit the first stitch and then let both slip off the left needle.

1/1 LC (Left Cross)
With the right needle *behind* the first stitch, knit the second stitch through the front strand, knit the first stitch the usual way, and then let both stitches slip off the left needle.

RT (Right Twist)
K2tog but do not drop stitches from the needle: Insert the right-hand needle between the stitches just knit together, and knit the first stitch again. Now slip both stitches together from the needle.

BODY

With the smaller needle, cast on 112 (120, 128, 132, 144) stitches.

Knit 4 rows.

Change to larger needle. Place a marker A and join for working in the round.

Setup round: K5 (7, 9, 10, 13), place a marker B, work 45 stitches of the Camisole Lace pattern across, place a marker B, k5 (7, 9, 10, 13), place a marker A to indicate side seam, knit to the end.

Continue in pattern as established, working the Camisole Lace pattern between B markers, until the body measures 8½ (9, 9½, 11, 12)" (21.5 [23, 24, 28, 30.5]cm) from the cast-on edge, ending with an odd-numbered row.

FRONT

Work to 4 (5, 6, 7, 8) stitches from side seam marker, bind off 8 (10, 12, 14, 16) stitches, k7 and place these stitches on a holder, bind off 34 (36, 38, 38, 42) center back stitches, k7 and place these stitches on a holder, bind off 8 (10, 12, 14, 16) stitches—these include the first 4 (5, 6, 7, 8) stitches of the next round.

Row 1 (RS): Sl 1, k0 (1, 2, 2, 4), work the first 8 stitches of chart, ssk, work to 10 stitches before marker B, k2tog, work the last 8 stitches of the Camisole Lace Chart, k1 (2, 3, 3, 5)—46 (48, 50, 50, 54) stitches.

Row 2: Sl 1, p0 (1, 2, 2, 4), k2, p4, k2, purl to 8 stitches before marker B, k2, p4, k2, p1 (2, 3, 3, 5).

Repeat rows 1 and 2 until camisole measures 10 (10½, 11, 12½, 13½)" (25.5 [26.5, 28, 32, 34.5] cm) from the cast-on edge, ending with a right-side row—6 total decrease rows, 36 (38, 40, 40, 44) stitches.

front edging

Change to smaller needle.

Rows 1 and 3 (WS): Sl 1, p6, knit to the last 7 stitches, p7.

Rows 2 and 4: Sl 1, knit to the end.

Row 5: K7 and place these stitches on a holder, bind off the center 22 (24, 26, 26, 30) stitches, k7.

SHOULDER STRAPS (*make 2*)

With smaller needle, work strap on the last 7 stitches.

Row 1: K4; with yarn in front, slip the last 3 stitches purlwise.

Row 2: Give yarn a slight tug, k4; with yarn in front, slip the last 3 stiches purlwise.

Repeat row 2 until Strap measures 6 (6¼, 6¾, 7¼, 7¾)" (15 [15.5, 17, 18.5, 20]cm) or desired length.

Next row: Bind off 3 stitches; with yarn in front, slip last 3 stitches purlwise.

Next row: Bind off 3 stitches; cut yarn and pull through the last stitch.

FINISHING

Graft shoulder straps to back stitches on holders. Sew the bottom side seam. Weave in the ends. Block, if desired.

Camisole Lace Pattern

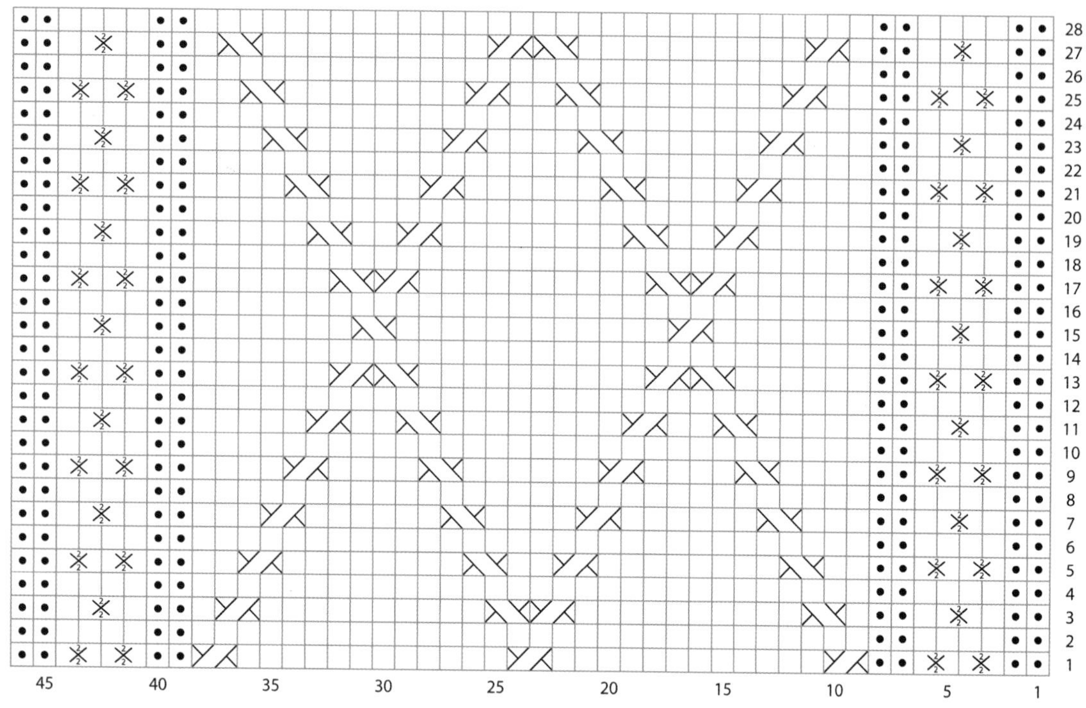

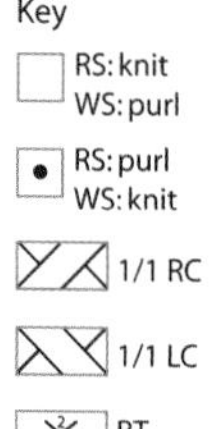

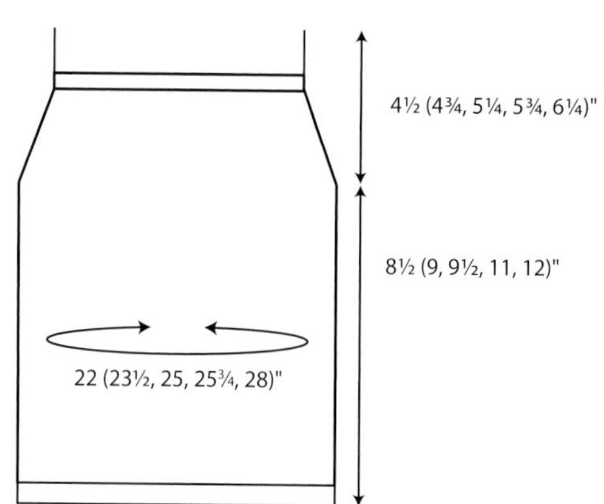

laura doll camisole

skill level

Intermediate

finished measurement

Chest circumference:
11-13" (28-33cm)

materials

- Sublime Baby Silk & Bamboo DK, 80% bamboo-sourced viscose, 20% silk; 1¾ oz (50g), 104 yd (95m); 1 ball in #270 (3)
- Size U.S. 5 (3.75mm) circular needle, 16" (40.5cm) length, or size to obtain gauge
- Size U.S. 3 (3.25mm) circular needle, 16" (40.5cm) length
- 4 stitch markers (2 of color A and 2 of color B)
- 3 stitch holders
- Darning needle

gauge

5 stitches and 7 rows = 1" (2.5cm) in stockinette stitch

BODY

With smaller needle, cast on 68 stitches.

Knit 4 rows.

Change to larger needle. Place a marker A and join for working in the round.

Setup round: K2, place a marker B, work 32 stitches of Doll Camisole Lace pattern, place a marker B, k2, place a marker A to indicate side seam, knit to the end.

Continue in pattern as established, working chart between B markers until 27 rounds of the pattern are complete.

FRONT

Work to 1 stitch before the side seam, bind off 2 stitches, k7 and place these stitches on a holder, bind off 18 center back stitches, k7 and place these stitches on a holder, bind off 2 stitches (includes beginning of the next round)—32 stitches.

Continue working back and forth in Doll Camisole Lace pattern until 37 rows of chart are complete.

front edging

Change to the smaller needle.

Row 1 (WS): Sl 1, p6, knit to the last 7 stitches, p7.

Row 2: Sl 1, knit to the end.

Row 3: P7 and place these stitches on a holder; bind off 18 stitches, p7.

SHOULDER STRAPS *(make 2)*

With smaller needle, work the shoulder strap on the last 7 stitches.

Row 1: K4; with yarn in front, slip the last 3 stitches purlwise.

Row 2: Give yarn a slight tug, k4, with yarn in front, slip the last 3 stitches purlwise.

Repeat row 2 until the strap measures 2" (5cm).

Place stitches on a holder.

FINISHING

Graft the shoulder straps to the back stitches on holders. Darn the bottom edge seam. Weave in the ends. Block, if desired.

Doll Camisole Lace Pattern

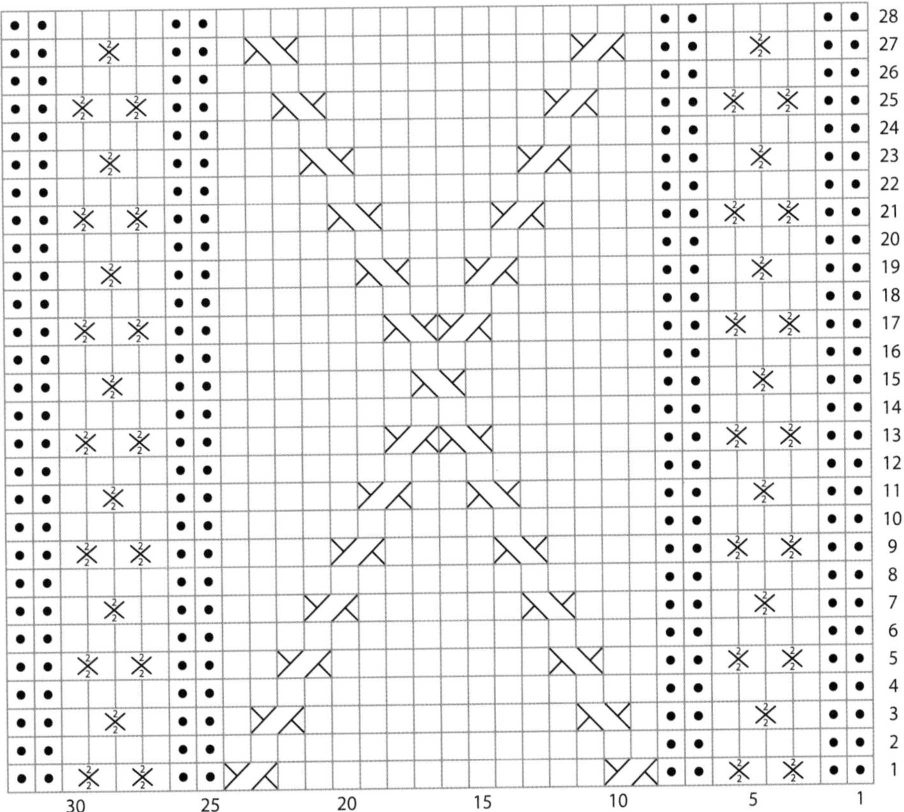

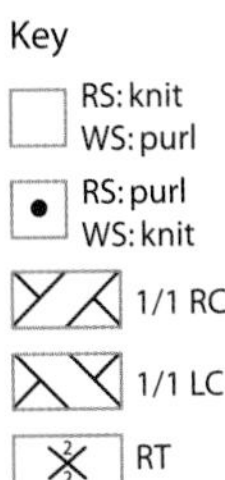

CHAPTER THREE accessories

One of my oldest daughter's favorite things to do is climb the fifteen-year-old magnolia tree that grows outside our gate. She's not quite big enough to climb on her own, but luckily the low branches are just the right height for dollies. When I think back to my childhood, I remember the trees just as well as I remember the dolls, maybe even more so. Sticks became swords, dirt piles became mountains, and (much to my mother's chagrin) mud puddles became moats in my imagination.

The projects in this chapter will remind you of the simple pleasures of outdoor play, whether it's an all-ages naptime below the branches with a blanket and pillow (Quinn Blanket, page 133) or a sweet little lad donning his felted crown and climbing as high as he might, declaring to the world that he is king (Grayson Felted Crown, page 110). A tree truly can be a limitless realm for the imagination, and every child should have the experience of ruling over a few.

grayson felted crown

All the little princes and princesses in your life will love these felted crowns, sure to make playtime fun. This crafty project combines knitting and hand sewing; the quick-to-knit crowns can be embroidered in the colors and themes of your choice. For a thicker fabric, double the yarn amounts required and hold two yarn strands together as you knit.

skill level
Easy

sizes
Doll (Toddler, Child).
Shown in Toddler.

finished measurements
Width: 16 (20, 22)" (40.5 [51, 56]cm)

materials

- Cascade 220, 100% Peruvian highland wool, 3½ oz (100g), 220 yd (201m); 1 (1, 1) skein in #8891 Cyan Blue (4)
- Size U.S. 9 (5.5mm) or U.S. 10 (6mm) needles
- Felted Crown template, page 112
- Copy paper and a piece of cardboard, about 8 x 10" (20.5 x 25.5cm)
- Darning needle
- Embroidery floss in assorted colors
- Size 22 embroidery needle
- Chalk
- Fabric glue, sequins, and glitter (optional)
- Elastic (optional)

gauge

Gauge is not necessary for this pattern. Using a larger needle than called for on the yarn ball band by about 2 needle sizes makes for larger stitches, which felt more easily.

notes

Refer to Special Stitches and Techniques (page 151) for instructions on the baseball stitch and page 140 for basic hand-stitch instructions.

FABRIC FOR CROWN

Cast on 25 stitches.

Work in garter stitch for 34 (40, 45)" (86 [101.5, 114]cm).

Bind off.

FELTING

Felt the piece following the instructions in How to Felt (page 115). Trim the bottom and side edges to straighten as necessary.

Enlarge the crown template on copy paper and trace the shape onto a piece of cardboard. Using chalk, retrace the shape as many times as necessary across the top of the crown. Cut the fabric to shape.

Cut the felted crown piece to measure 15½ (17, 19)" (39.5 [43, 48.5]cm) or desired length. **Note:** Add 1" (2.5cm) to the actual head circumference of your doll or child.

FINISHING

Use the baseball stitch to secure the two ends together with embroidery floss.

Decorate the crown as desired. Kids may love using fabric glue, sequins, glitter, and beads to cover their crowns in pretty "jewels." I used an embroidery needle and floss to add blanket stitch along the bottom edge; back stitch to create circles, stars, and swirls; and satin stitch to make solid circles that look like small round jewels.

tip: If the crown is too small to fit your child or doll, cut open the back and sew 1-2" (2.5-5cm) of elastic across the opening. Doll head sizes vary greatly, so this may ensure that the crown fits multiple dolls.

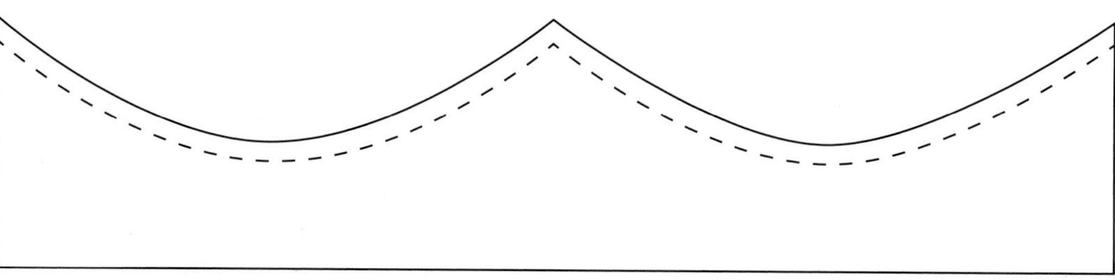

Felted Crown Template: Trace curves with chalk onto felt.

HOW TO FELT

Felt the knit crown fabric using a washing machine set to hot and the roughest wash cycle. (Don't select delicate, you *want* the wool to get pushed around a lot!) Check on the knit piece every ten minutes or so during the wash cycle to see how you like the resulting fabric. You may want to knit and felt a swatch first, to test how your machine felts the yarn you have selected. I like for the fabric to look as dense and smooth as possible. The garter stitch pattern of the crown results in a ribbed effect; work in stockinette stitch if you prefer a smoother fabric.

Stop your washing machine before it goes into the spin cycle and clean up any excess fiber that has fuzzed off during the wash cycles. This will prevent your machine from becoming clogged up. Then allow the machine to go into the spin cycle. (Using the machine at this step does risk clogging, but I'm a rebel). Remove the piece from the machine and roll it in a towel to squeeze any excess water remaining. Block flat to the finished measurement on a blocking board. Ta-da! You have created your very own felt fabric.

samantha lace kneesocks

I just can't resist a little girl in kneesocks! These lace lattice motif socks can be styled classically, with a sweet pair of Mary Janes, or look oh-so-modern when peeking out from boots. They're so cute, you'll want to knit a pair of these incredibly sweet kneesocks, sized all the way up to a Women's 7, for every lady on your list.

skill level
Intermediate

sizes
Child's Shoe Size 4-8 (7-11, 10-2, 2-4), Women's 5-7

finished measurements
Foot circumference: 5 (5¾, 6¼, 6¾, 8)" (12.5 [14.5, 15.5, 17, 20.5]cm)
Foot length: 5 (6, 7½, 8, 8½)" (12.5 [15, 19, 20.5, 21.5]cm)
Cuff circumference: 6½ (7, 8, 8½, 9½)" (16.5 [18, 20.5, 21.5, 24]cm)
Leg length (cuff to top of heel): 10½ (11½, 12½, 13½, 15)" (26.5 [29.5, 32, 34.5, 38]cm)

materials

- SweetGeorgia Superwash Sock, 100% superwash merino wool, 4 oz (114g), 375 yd (343m); 1 skein in China Doll (1)
- Size U.S. 1 (2.25mm) needles for working in the round, or size to obtain gauge
- 3 stitch markers
- Darning needle

gauge

28 stitches and 40 rounds = 4" (10cm) in stockinette stitch

notes

You can use your favorite top-down sock knitting technique for this pattern. Choose double-pointed needles, one long circular needle, or 2 short circular needles, according to your preference.

Refer to Special Stitches and Techniques (page 151) for instructions on the three-needle bind-off and grafting stitches.

LEG

Cast on 46 (50, 56, 60, 68) stitches. Distribute stitches across needles as needed, place a marker, and join for working in the round.

Ribbing round: *K1 through the back loop, p1; repeat from * around.

Repeat Ribbing round for 1 (1, 1, 1, 2)" (2.5 [2.5, 2.5, 2.5, 5]cm).

Left Sock Only

K8 (9, 10, 11, 12), place a marker, work round 1 of the Lace Panel (see page 120) over 11 stitches, place a marker, knit to the end.

The leg is worked in stockinette stitch with the Lace Panel between markers as set.

Right Sock Only

K27 (30, 35, 38, 45), place a marker, work round 1 of the Lace Panel over 11 stitches, place a marker, knit to the end.

lace panel pattern

Note: This pattern is also in chart form on page 118.

Round 1: P2, k2tog, [k1, yarn over] twice, k1, [sl 1, k1, pass slipped stitch over (skp)], p2.

Rounds 2, 4, and 6: P2, k7, p2.

Round 3: P2, k2tog, yarn over, k3, yarn over, skp, p2.

Round 5: P2, k1, yarn over, skp, k1, k2tog, yarn over, k1, p2.

Round 7: P2, k2, yarn over, [sl 1, k2tog, pass slipped stitch over (sk2p)], yarn over, k2, p2.

Round 8: Repeat round 2.

Work 11 (11, 11, 15, 11) rounds even in pattern as set.

Shaping round: K1, ssk, work in pattern as set to 3 stitches before the end of the round, k2tog, k1—2 stitches decreased.

Continuing in pattern, work Shaping round every 15 (17, 15, 17, 17) rounds 4 (4, 5, 5, 5) times more—36 (40, 44, 48, 56) stitches.

Work even in pattern until leg measures 10½ (11½, 12½, 13½, 15)" (26.5 [29.5, 32, 34.5, 38] cm) from the cast-on edge, ending 9 (10, 11, 12, 14) stitches before the end of the round on round 8 of the Lace Panel stitch pattern. This will now be the new start of the round.

Stitch markers for the lace panel may be removed.

HEEL FLAP

The heel flap will be worked flat on the first 18 (20, 22, 24, 28) stitches of the round.

Row 1 (RS): *Sl 1, k1; repeat from * 8 (9, 10, 11, 13) times more, turn.

Row 2: Sl 1, p17 (19, 21, 23, 27), turn.

Repeat the last two rows 6 (7, 8, 9, 11) times more, then work row 1 once more.

TURN HEEL

Row 1 (WS): P10 (11, 12, 13, 15), p2tog, p1, turn.

Row 2: Sl 1, k3, skp, k1, turn.

Row 3: Sl 1, p4, p2tog, p1, turn.

Row 4: Sl 1, k5, skp, k1, turn.

Row 5: Sl 1, p6, p2tog, p1, turn.

Row 6: Sl 1, k7, skp, k1, turn.

Child 4-8 Only

Row 7: Sl 1, p8, p2tog, turn.

Row 8: K9, skp–10 stitches remain.

Child 7-11 Only

Row 7: Sl 1, p8, p2tog, p1, turn.

Row 8: Sl 1, k9, skp, k1, turn–12 stitches remain.

Child 10-2 Only

Row 7: Sl 1, p8, p2tog, p1, turn.

Row 8: Sl 1, k9, skp, k1, turn.

Row 9: Sl 1, p10, p2tog, turn.

Row 10: K11, skp–12 stitches remain.

Child 2-4 Only

Row 7: Sl 1, p8, p2tog, p1, turn.

Row 8: Sl 1, k9, skp, k1, turn.

Row 9: Sl 1, p10, p2tog, p1, turn.

Row 10: Sl 1, k11, skp, k1, turn–14 stitches remain.

Women 5-7 Only

Row 7: Sl 1, p8, p2tog, p1, turn.

Row 8: Sl 1, k9, skp, k1, turn.

Row 9: Sl 1, p10, p2tog, p1, turn.

Row 10: Sl 1, k11, skp, k1, turn.

Row 11: Sl 1, p12, p2tog, p1, turn.

Row 12: Sl 1, k13, skp, k1–16 stitches remain.

GUSSET

With the right-side facing, pick up and knit 9 (10, 11, 12, 14) stitches along the first side of the heel flap, using the slipped stitches as a guide. Place a marker and k18 (20, 22, 24, 28) stitches of instep, place a marker. Pick up and knit 9 (10, 11, 12, 14) stitches along the second side of the heel flap, using the slipped stitches as a guide. K5 (6, 6, 7, 8) stitches of heel, place a marker–46 (52, 56, 62, 72) stitches. This is the new start of round. Rearrange stitches on your needles as needed.

Round 1: Knit.

Round 2: Knit to 3 stitches before the marker, k2tog, k1; knit to the next marker; k1, ssk, knit to the end.

Repeat the last 2 rounds 4 (5, 5, 6, 7) times more–36 (40, 44, 48, 56) stitches.

FOOT

Work even in stockinette stitch until the sock foot measures 3¾ (4¾, 6, 6½, 6½)" (9.5 [12, 15, 16.5, 16.5]cm) from the back of the heel, or 1 (1¼, 1½, 1½, 2)" (2.5 [3, 3.8, 3.8, 5]cm) less than the desired length.

toe shaping

Round 1: [Knit to 3 stitches before the marker, k2tog, k2, ssk] twice, knit to the end—4 stitches decreased.

Round 2: Knit.

Repeat rounds 1 and 2 until 20 (24, 24, 28, 32) stitches remain.

Repeat round 1 until 8 stitches remain.

Close the toe using the three-needle bind-off, or graft the stitches together.

finishing

Weave in the ends. Block, if desired.

Lace Panel

	10				5				1	
•	•								•	•	8
•	•			○	∧	○			•	•	7
•	•								•	•	6
•	•		○	/		\	○		•	•	5
•	•								•	•	4
•	•	\	○				○	/	•	•	3
•	•								•	•	2
•	•	\		○		○		/	•	•	1

Key

- ☐ knit
- • purl
- / k2tog
- \ slt, k1, psso
- ○ yo
- ∧ sk2p

samantha doll lace kneesocks

skill level
Intermediate

finished measurement
Leg circumference:
Approximately 5½" (14cm)

materials
- SweetGeorgia Superwash Sock, 100% superwash merino wool, 4 oz (114g), 375 yd (343m); 100 yd (91m) in China Doll (1)
- Size U.S. 1 (2.25mm) circular needle, 32 or 40" (81 or 101.5cm) length, or size to obtain gauge
- 3 stitch markers
- Darning needle

gauge
7 stitches and 10 rounds = 1" (2.5cm) in stockinette stitch

notes
The shape and size of doll feet vary among manufacturers, so I've written this pattern to fit the most widely available handmade cloth dolls. The pattern will probably fit a few of your child's stuffed animals as well. The finished socks do not have heels because many cloth dolls do not have a turn in their feet.

For the Lace Panel instructions and chart, see pages 116 and 118.

Refer to Special Stitches and Techniques (page 151) for instructions on the three-needle bind-off and grafting stitches.

LEG
Cast on 46 stitches. Place a marker and join for working in the round.

Ribbing round: *K1 through the back loop, p1; repeat from * around.

Repeat Ribbing round for 1" (2.5cm).

Left Sock Only

Next round: K7, place a marker, work 11 stitches of the Lace Panel pattern (page 116), place a marker, knit to the end.

Right Sock Only

Next round: K28, place a marker, work 11 stitches of the Lace Panel pattern, place a marker, knit to the end.

For Both Socks

Continue even in stockinette stitch, working the Lace Panel pattern between markers, until 16 rows of the lace pattern have been completed.

FAUX INSTEP
Rounds 1 and 2: Knit.

Round 3: Purl.

Round 4: K13, k2tog, k16, ssk, k13—44 stitches remain.

Rounds 5, 7, 9, 11, and 13: Knit.
Round 6: K12, k2tog, k16, ssk, k12–42 stitches remain.
Round 8: K11, k2tog, k16, ssk, k11–40 stitches remain.
Round 10: K10, k2tog, k16, ssk, k10–38 stitches remain.
Round 12: K9, k2tog, k16, ssk, k9–36 stitches remain.
Round 14: K8, k2tog, k16, ssk, k8–34 stitches remain.

FAUX TOE

Round 1: K6, ssk, k1, k2tog, k12, ssk, k1, k2tog, k6–30 stitches remain.
Rounds 2, 4, and 6: Knit.
Round 3: K5, ssk, k1, k2tog, k10, ssk, k1, k2tog, k5–26 stitches remain.
Round 5: K4, ssk, k1, k2tog, k8, ssk, k1, k2tog, k4–22 stitches remain.
Round 7: K3, ssk, k1, k2tog, k6, ssk, k1, k2tog, k3–18 stitches remain.
Round 8: Knit.
K5; this is now the new end of the round.
Arrange the stitches so the first and last 9 stitches are on each of two needles.
Close the toe using the three-needle bind-off, or graft the stitches together.

FINISHING

Weave in the ends. Block, if desired.

james mixed-up socks

The simple stockinette stitch sock never goes out of style—for big and little kids alike. This delightful pattern offers choices for knee-length or standard length socks in a solid color or whatever crazy striped combinations you like. Mix them up in whichever combination suits you, as they will be off the needles—and you'll be ready to start a new pair—in no time.

materials

- Madelinetosh Sock, 100% superwash merino wool, 4 oz (114g), 395 yd (361m); Solid color socks: 1 skein each in Alabaster (MC) and Fig (CC); Striped kneesocks: 1 skein each in Fragrant (MC), Alabaster (CC) 1
- Size U.S. 1 (2.25mm) needles for working in the round, or size to obtain gauge
- 2 stitch markers
- Darning needle
- Smooth waste yarn in a contrasting color

gauge

28 stitches and 40 rounds = 4" (10cm) in stockinette stitch

notes

You can use your favorite top-down sock knitting technique for this pattern. Choose double-pointed needles, one long circular needle, or 2 short circular needles, according to your preference.

Refer to Special Stitches and Techniques (page 151) for instructions on the k1, p1 rib, three-needle bind-off, and grafting stitches.

skill level

Intermediate

sizes

Child's Shoe Size 4-8 (7-11, 10-2, 2-4), Women's 5-7

finished measurements

Foot circumference: 5 (5¾, 6¼, 6¾, 8)" (12.5 [14.5, 15.5, 17, 20.5]cm)

Foot length: 5 (6, 7½, 8, 8½)" (12.5 [15, 19, 20.5, 21.5]cm)

Cuff circumference: 6½ (7, 8, 8½, 9½)" (16.5 [18, 20.5, 21.5, 24]cm)

Leg length (cuff to top of heel): 4 (4½, 5, 5½, 6½)" (10 [11.5, 12.5, 14, 16.5]cm) for solid color socks; 10½ (11½, 12½, 13½, 15)" (26.5 [29.5, 32, 34.5, 38]cm) for striped kneesocks

LEG

Solid Color Socks

Using MC, cast on 36 (40, 44, 48, 56) stitches. Distribute stitches across needles as needed, place a marker, and join for working in the round.

Work in k1, p1 rib for 1 (1, 1, 1, 2)" (2.5 [2.5, 2.5, 2.5, 5]cm).

Cut MC, join CC. Work even in stockinette stitch until leg measures 4 (4½, 5, 5½, 6½)" (10 [11.5, 12.5, 14, 16.5]cm), or desired length from the cast-on edge. Skip to Heel Placement.

Striped Kneesocks

Using MC, cast on 46 (50, 56, 60, 68) stitches. Distribute stitches across needles as needed, place a marker, and join for working in the round.

Work in k1, p1 rib for 1 (1, 1, 1, 2)" (2.5 [2.5, 2.5, 2.5, 5]cm).

The remainder of the sock is worked in stockinette stitch in the following stripe pattern: 20 rounds CC, 20 rounds MC.

Join CC and work 12 (12, 12, 16, 16) rounds in stripe pattern.

Shaping round: K1, ssk, knit to 3 stitches before the end of the round, k2tog, k1–2 stitches decreased.

Work 14 (16, 14, 16, 16) rounds even in stripe pattern.

Continue in stripe pattern as set, repeat the last 15 (17, 15, 17, 17) rounds 4 (4, 5, 5, 5) times more–36 (40, 44, 48, 56) stitches.

Work even in stripe pattern until leg measures 10½ (11½, 12½, 13½, 15)" (26.5 [29.5, 32, 34.5, 38]cm) from the cast-on edge, ending the final round 9 (10, 11, 12, 14) stitches before the end of the round. This will now be the new start of round. Rearrange stitches on the needles as needed.

The first 18 (20, 22, 24, 28) stitches of the round form the heel, the last 18 (20, 22, 24, 28) stitches of the round form the instep.

HEEL PLACEMENT

With waste yarn, k18 (20, 22, 24, 28) and slip these stitches back onto the needle.

FOOT

Continue in pattern as set, until sock foot measures 3 (3¾, 4¾, 5, 4¾)" (7.5 [9.5, 12, 12.5, 12]cm) from waste yarn, or 2 (2¼, 2¾, 3, 3¾)" (5 [5.5, 7, 7.5, 9.5]cm) short of desired foot length.

toe shaping

Note: For solid color socks, change to MC. For striped kneesocks, continue in stripe pattern, changing colors as required.

Round 1: K18 (20, 22, 24, 28), place a second marker, knit to the end.

Round 2: *K1, ssk, knit to 3 stitches before the

marker, k2tog, k1; repeat from * once more—4 stitches decreased.

Round 3: Knit.

Repeat rounds 2 and 3 until 20 (24, 24, 28, 32) stitches remain.

Repeat round 2 until 8 stitches remain.

Close the toe with the three-needle bind-off, or graft the stitches together.

HEEL SHAPING

Carefully remove the waste yarn that marks the heel stitches, and place the stitches onto your needles—18 (20, 22, 24, 28) stitches on the back of the heel and 17 (19, 21, 23, 27) stitches on the front of the heel. Distribute the stitches on your needles as needed, place a marker, and join for working in the round with MC at start of front heel stitches.

Round 1: K17 (19, 21, 23, 27), place a second marker, knit to the end.

Round 2: K14 (16, 18, 20, 24), k2tog, k2, ssk, k12 (14, 18, 20, 24), k2tog, k1—32 (36, 40, 44, 52) stitches.

Round 3: Knit.

Round 4: *K1, ssk, knit to 3 stitches before the marker, k2tog, k1; repeat from * once more—4 stitches decreased.

Repeat rounds 3 and 4 until 16 stitches remain.

Knit 1 round.

FINISHING

Close heel with the three-needle bind-off, or graft the stitches together. Weave in the ends. Block, if desired.

james doll mixed-up socks

skill level
Intermediate

finished measurement
Leg circumference:
Approximately 5½" (14cm)

materials

- Madelinetosh Sock, 100% superwash merino wool, 4 oz (114g), 395 yd (361m); 100 yd (91m) in Alabaster, or any leftover sock yarn remnants (1)
- Size U.S. 1 (2.25mm) circular needle, 32 or 40" (81 or 101.5cm) lengths, or size to obtain gauge
- 2 stitch markers
- Darning needle

gauge

7 stitches and 10 rows = 1" (2.5cm) in stockinette stitch

notes

The shape and size of doll feet vary among manufacturers, so I've written this pattern to fit the most widely available handmade cloth dolls. The pattern will probably fit a few of your child's stuffed animals as well. The finished socks do not have heels because many cloth dolls do not have a turn in their feet.

Refer to Special Stitches and Techniques (page 151) for instructions on the three-needle bind-off and grafting stitches.

LEG

Cast on 46 stitches. Place a marker and join for working in the round.

Ribbing round: *K1 through the back loop, p1; repeat from * around.

Repeat Ribbing round for 1" (2.5cm).

Work in stockinette stitch for 1½" (3.8cm).

FAUX INSTEP

Round 1: Purl.

Round 2: K13, k2tog, k16, ssk, k13—44 stitches remain.

Rounds 3, 5, 7, 9, and 11: Knit.

Round 4: K12, k2tog, k16, ssk, k12—42 stitches remain.

Round 6: K11, k2tog, k16, ssk, k11—40 stitches remain.

Round 8: K10, k2tog, k16, ssk, k10—38 stitches remain.

Round 10: K9, k2tog, k16, ssk, k9—36 stitches remain.

Round 12: K8, k2tog, k16, ssk, k8—34 stitches remain.

Round 13: Knit.

FAUX TOE

Round 14: K6, ssk, place a marker, k1, k2tog, k12, ssk, k1, k2tog, k6—30 stitches remain.

Rounds 15, 17, 19, and 21: Knit.

Round 16: K5, ssk, k1, k2tog, k10, ssk, k1, k2tog, k5—26 stitches remain.

Round 18: K4, ssk, k1, k2tog, k8, ssk, k1, k2tog, k4—22 stitches remain.

Round 20: K3, ssk, k1, k2tog, k6, ssk, k1, k2tog, k3—18 stitches remain.

Round 22: K5; this is now the new end of round.

Arrange the stitches so the first and last 9 stitches are on each of two needles.

Close the toe using the three-needle bind-off, or graft the stitches together.

FINISHING

Weave in the ends. Block, if desired.

rowan owl hat

This hat started as a swatch for the Ari Owl Sweater (page 36), a pattern I was working on in honor of my younger daughter's love for owls. The name for this bird was one of her first words. Now she wants to wear the hat whenever we leave the house, and hearing her sweet little two-year-old voice asking for, "mah owl hat, Momma!" is music to my ears.

skill level
Intermediate

sizes
Baby (Toddler, Child, Adult). Shown in size Toddler.

finished measurements
Circumference: 18 (19½, 21¼, 23)" (45.5 [49.5, 54, 58.5]cm)

materials

- Lorna's Laces Shepherd Worsted, 100% superwash merino wool, 4 oz (114g), 225 yd (206m); 1 skein Natural (A); 50 yd (46m) each in Harvest (B), Solitude (C), Whisper (D), and Old Rose (E) (4)
- Size U.S. 6 (4mm) double-pointed needles, or size to obtain gauge, plus circular needle if using the Magic Loop method
- Stitch marker
- Darning needle

gauge

5½ stitches and 6½ rows = 1" (2.5cm) in stockinette stitch in the round

notes

Refer to Special Stitches and Techniques (page 151) for instructions on the k1, p1 rib, the backward-loop cast-on, and Magic Loop method. If using Lorna's Laces Shepherd Worsted yarn, I do not recommend machine drying after washing. Although it is a superwash merino wool yarn, the heat may affect the two-color rounds differently from the rest of the sweater and may distort the design.

special stitch

Corrugated rib

Round 1: *K1 A, p1 B; repeat from * around.

HAT

With A, cast on 94 (100, 106, 110) stitches. Place a marker and join for working in the round.

Round 1: *K1, p1, repeat from *.

Rounds 2-7 (corrugated rib): *K1 A, p1 B; repeat from * around.

Increase round: With A, *k18 (12, 9, 6), m1 using the backward-loop cast-on; repeat from * to the last 4 (4, 7, 14) stitches, knit to the end—99 (108, 117, 126) stitches.

With A, work even in stockinette stitch for 1" (2.5cm).

Work 2 rounds of Owl Hat Chart A, ending with stitch 3 (4, 1, 2), then work 14 rounds of Owl Hat Chart B.

With A, continue even in stockinette stitch until hat measures 6½ (7½, 8, 8½)" (16.5 [19, 20.5, 21.5]cm) from the cast-on edge.

Change to double-pointed needles when stitches no longer fit around the circular needle.

CROWN DECREASES

Round 1: K1 (0, 1, 0), *k2tog; repeat from * around—50 (54, 59, 63) stitches.

Rounds 2, 4, and 6: Knit.

Round 3: K0 (0, 1, 1), *k2tog; repeat from * around—25 (27, 30, 32) stitches.

Round 5: K1 (1, 0, 0), *k2tog; repeat from * around—13 (14, 15, 16) stitches.

Round 7: K1 (0, 1, 0), *k2tog; repeat from * around—7 (7, 8, 8) stitches.

Cut yarn, leaving a 6" (15cm) tail. Thread tail through the remaining stitches, pull tight, and weave in the end on the inside of the hat. I suggest leaving 2" (5cm) of the tail sticking out on the inside for a secure finish.

Owl Hat

Chart A

 A Natural

 B Harvest

C Solitude

 D Whisper

 E Old Rose

Chart B

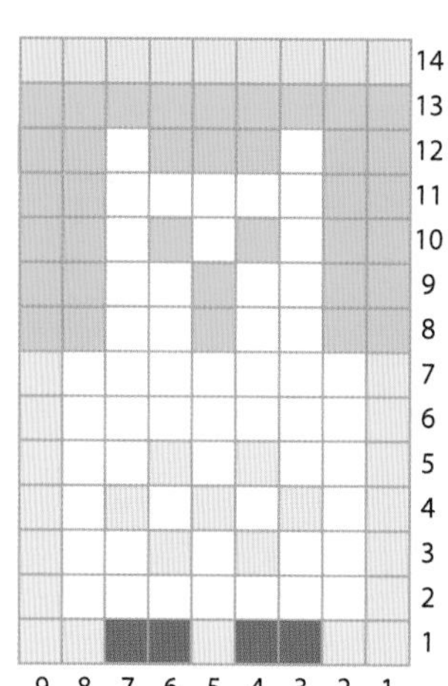

rowan doll owl hat

skill level

Intermediate

finished measurement

Head circumference: 14" (37cm)

materials

- Lorna's Laces Shepherd Worsted, 100% superwash merino wool, 4 oz (114g), 225 yd (206m); 100 yd (91m) in Natural (A); 50 yd (46m) each in Harvest (B), Solitude (C), Whisper (D), and Old Rose (E) (4)
- Size U.S. 6 (4mm) double-pointed needles or circular needle for Magic Loop method, or size to obtain gauge
- Stitch marker
- Darning needle

gauge

5½ stitches and 6½ rows = 1" (2.5cm) in stockinette stitch in the round

notes

To adjust the hat's circumference, cast on 9 fewer, or more, stitches to accommodate the owl pattern, which is 9 stitches wide and measures almost 2" (5cm). Make the hat deeper or more shallow by knitting more or fewer more plain rounds after the owl chart.

notes *(continued)*

Refer to Special Stitches and Techniques (page 151) for instructions on the k1, p1 rib, and Magic Loop method.

If using Lorna's Laces Shepherd Worsted yarn, I do not recommend machine drying after washing. Although it is a superwash merino wool yarn, the heat may affect the two-color rounds differently from the rest of the sweater and may distort the design.

special stitch

Corrugated rib

Round 1: *K1 A, p1 B; repeat from * around.

HAT

With A, cast on 80 stitches. Place a marker and join for working in the round.

Round 1: *K1, p1, repeat from *.

Rounds 2-6: *K1 A, p1 B; repeat from * around.

Increase round: With A, *knit through the front and back of the stitch (kfb), k7; repeat from * around—90 stitches.

Knit 1 round with A.

Work 2 rounds of Owl Hat Chart A, ending with stitch 2, then work 12 rounds of Owl Hat Chart B.

Next round: *K7, k2tog; repeat from * around—80 stitches.

Work round 14 of Owl Hat Chart B.

With A, continue even in stockinette stitch for 1½" (3.8cm).

CROWN DECREASES

Decrease round: *K2tog; repeat from * around.

Continue in stockinette stitch, repeat Decrease round every 2nd row twice more—10 stitches remain.

Cut yarn, leaving a 6" (15cm) tail. Thread tail through the remaining stitches, pull tight, and weave in the end.

quinn blanket

I'll admit it: I'm picky when it comes to knitting blankets. They need to be simple enough to work mindlessly but without boredom, and they need to look nice from both sides. For me, the Quinn Blanket has it all—a few color changes and rows of openwork stitches quickly create a lovely pile of colors in a fun ripple pattern.

skill level
Easy

sizes
Doll (Child)

finished measurements
Approximately 20 (36½)" (51 [92.5]cm) square

materials

- Spud & Chloë Sweater, 55% superwash wool, 45% organic cotton, 3½ oz (100g), 160 yd (146m); 1 (3) skeins in #7500 Ice Cream (A); 1 (2) skeins in #7518 Barn (B); 1 (1) skein each in #7508 Pollen (C), #7502 Grass (D), and #7510 Splash (E) (4)
- Size U.S. 9 (5.5mm) circular needle, at least 24" (61cm) length, or size to obtain gauge
- 7 (14) stitch markers (optional)

gauge

4½ stitches = 1" (2.5cm) in garter stitch

special stitches

Ripple Stitch *(multiple of 11 stitches)*

Row 1 (RS): *K2tog, k2, [knit through the front and back of the next stitch (kfb)] twice, k3, ssk; repeat from * to end.

Contrast Ripple with A

Rows 1 and 3 (RS): Ripple Stitch.

Rows 2 and 4: Knit.

Color Ripple with B–E

Row 1 (RS): Ripple Stitch.

Rows 2–6: Knit.

BLANKET

With B cast on 88 (165) stitches.

Work Color Ripple with B.

Work Contrast Ripple with A.

Work Color Ripple with C.

Work Contrast Ripple with A.

Work Color Ripple with D.

Work Contrast Ripple with A.

Work Color Ripple with E.

Work Contrast Ripple with A.

Continue working pattern in color sequence as established until blanket measures just short of 18 (36)" (45.5 [91]cm) long, ending with a Contrast Ripple.

BOTTOM EDGE

With B work as follows:

Rows 1 and 3 (RS): Ripple Stitch.

Rows 2 and 4: Knit.

Bind off loosely.

FINISHING

Weave in the ends. Block, if desired.

jesse bear hat

Make getting suited up for the heavy winter months more fun with this cute bear hat, a cure-all for cold-weather complaints. I've designed the pattern in three basic size ranges, from toddler through adult, so whether you are knitting for a Momma Bear, Poppa Bear, or Baby Bear, you'll be sure to find the size that's just right.

skill level
Easy

sizes
Toddler (Child, Adult)

finished measurements
Circumference: 20 (21¼, 22½)" (51 [54, 57.5]cm)

materials

- Nobori by Noro, 42% cotton, 31% nylon, 14% wool, 13% silk, 3½ oz (100g), 182 yd (166.4m); 1 (2, 2) skeins in #5 Blues, Pinks, Greens (5)
- Size U.S. 9 (5.5mm) circular needle, 40" (101.5cm) length, for Magic Loop method or set of 4 double-pointed needles, or size to obtain gauge
- 2 stitch markers
- Darning needle

gauge

3 stitches and 5 rows = 1" (2.5cm) in seed stitch

HAT

Cast on 60 (64, 68) stitches. Place a marker and join for working in the round.

Round 1: *K1, p1; repeat from * around.

Round 2: *P1, k1; repeat from * around.

Repeat rounds 1 and 2 for seed stitch until hat measures 6½ (7½, 8½)" (16.5 [19, 21.5]cm) from the cast-on edge.

CROWN DECREASES

Round 1: *K2tog, p1; repeat from * to the last 0 (1, 2) stitches, k0 (1, 1), p0 (0, 1)—40 (43, 46) stitches.
Round 2: *P1, k1; repeat from * to the last 0 (1, 0) stitch, p0 (1, 0).
Round 3: *P2tog, k1; repeat from * to the last stitch, p1—27 (29, 31) stitches.
Round 4: *K1, p1; repeat from * to the last stitch, k1.
Round 5: *K2tog, p2tog; repeat from * to the last 3 (1, 3) stitches, k2tog 1 (0, 1) time, p1—14 (15, 16) stitches.
Round 6: *P1, k1; repeat from * to the last 0 (1, 0) stitch, p0 (1, 0).
Round 7: *K2tog; repeat from * to the last 0 (1, 0) stitch, k0 (1, 0)—7 (8, 8) stitches.
Cut yarn, leaving an 8" (20.5cm) tail. Thread the tail through the remaining stitches, pull tight to close opening, and weave in the end.

EARS (*make 2*)

Note: Create m1 increases by picking up the bar between the stitches to be knit and then knitting into the back loop.
Starting at the tip of the ear, cast on 5 stitches.
Row 1 (RS): K1, *p1, k1; repeat from * to end.
Row 2: P1, m1, p1, k1, p1, m1, p1—7 stitches.
Row 3: P1, *k1, p1; repeat from * to end.
Row 4: K1, m1, [k1, p1] twice, k1, m1, k1—9 stitches.
Row 5: K1, *p1, k1; repeat from * to end.
Rows 6–9: Work in seed stitch as established.
Bind off in pattern.

Note: For a neater bind-off corner, work the last two stitches together before passing the previous stitch over.

FINISHING

With the cast-on tail indicating the center back of the hat, position the ears 4 (4½, 5)" (10 [11.5, 12.5]cm) apart at the top of the hat (as pictured) and whipstitch them into place. Weave in the ends.

tip: Be consistent when attaching the bear ears, sewing both onto the hat from the same side, in the same way. The ears will tilt differently, depending on the way you seam.

jesse doll bear hat

skill level

Easy

finished measurement

Circumference 15" (38cm)

materials

- Nobori by Noro; 42% cotton, 31% nylon, 14% wool, 13% silk, 3½ oz (100g), 182 yd (166.4m); 1 skein in #5 Blues, Pinks, Greens (5)
- Size U.S. 9 (5.5mm) double-pointed needles or size to obtain gauge
- 2 stitch markers
- Darning needle

gauge

3 stitches and 5 rows = 1" (2.5cm) in seed stitch

HAT

Cast on 45 stitches. Place a marker and join for working in the round.

Round 1: *K1, p1; repeat from * around.

Round 2: *P1, k1; repeat from * around.

Repeat rounds 1 and 2 for seed stitch until hat measures 3½" (9cm) from the cast-on edge.

CROWN DECREASES

Round 1: *K2tog, p1; repeat from * around—30 stitches.

Round 2: *P1, k1; repeat from * around.

Round 3: *P2tog, k1; repeat from * around—20 stitches.

Round 4: *K1, p1; repeat from * around.

Round 5: *K2tog, p2tog; repeat from * around—10 stitches.

Cut yarn, leaving an 8" (20.5cm) tail. Thread yarn through remaining stitches, pull tight to close opening, and weave in the end.

EARS (*make 2*)

Note: Create m1 increases by picking up the bar between the stitches to be knit and then knitting into the back loop.

Starting at the tip of the ear, cast on 5 stitches.

Row 1 (RS): K1, *p1, k1; repeat from * to end.

Row 2: P1, m1, p1, k1, p1, m1, p1—7 stitches.

Row 3: P1, *k1, p1; repeat from * to end.

Row 4: K1, m1, k1, [p1, k1] twice, m1, k1—9 stitches.

Row 5: K1, *p1, k1; repeat from * to end.

Rows 6-9: Continue in seed stitch as established.

Bind off in pattern.

FINISHING

With the cast-on tail indicating the center back of hat, position the ears 3½" (9cm) apart at the top of the hat (as pictured) and whipstitch them into place.

Weave in the ends. Block, if desired.

Just Like Me Sewing

It's one thing to knit matching sweaters for your child and their doll, but it's another to easily put them in matching jeans and T-shirts. Despite my lack of sewing experience, I was determined to solve that problem, for myself and for you. In the pages that follow, you'll find five easy patterns—the Ribbon Dress, the Ruffle Skirt, the Leggings, the T-Shirt, and the Jeans. My instructions are for machine sewing, but for all the sewn items in this book you may choose to skip the sewing machine. An introductory guide to hand stitches begins below.

There is an amazing feeling of accomplishment that comes from seeing a little doll all kitted out from head to toe in clothing created by your own hands. These beginner-level patterns will outfit any doll or toy with modern appeal and without breaking the bank. You even may be motivated to sew something for your child as well, and won't they be delighted?

Fabric Choices

The weight of a fabric affects the drape of any garment, but the effects can seem particularly dramatic on such small pieces as doll clothing. In general, thin fabric seems to work best. It curves around the body, stays reasonably wrinkle-free, and is especially forgiving to hand sewers. Little hands also seem to more easily put on doll clothing made with thinner fabrics.

Quilter's cotton fabrics come in the most wonderful patterns and in bundled assortments of precut fat quarters (18 × 22 inches [45.5 × 56cm]), but be careful if choosing this fabric. Some quilting cottons are thicker than others and may not be suited to clothing. I love high-quality sewing cotton for clothing. You will find a list of designers in the Resources section of the book for reference. Keep in mind that when sewing with cotton fabrics, it is also best to sew with cotton thread.

Two of the patterns in this book, the Leggings and the T-Shirt (pages 147 and 145), are made with knit fabric. When choosing a knit, look for one with a good bit of "stretchiness" in both directions. Any proper sewing book will advise you to use a ballpoint needle in your machine or possibly a different foot when sewing knit fabrics. However, I often forget to change my needle or foot, and it all works itself out. Don't worry too much about the rules, just start sewing! If you find yourself frustrated when working with these fabrics, you may want to try the specialty needle or foot.

Sewing Patterns

Each pattern piece includes a ¼" (6mm) seam allowance, so you don't have to do any extra measuring before cutting out the patterns. Some patterns include fold lines. Where indicated, fold the fabric before cutting it, and place the fold line on the same side as the icon. Then cut out the fabric. You are ready to sew!

Hand Sewing

If machine-sewing intimidates you, then you may find that such small projects as doll clothes are perfect for sewing by hand. There is a particular amount of pride that comes from hand-stitching—just as in knitting. Using a machine will be faster in some cases, but I've found that some tiny items, such as the cuff of a small sleeve, are much easier to sew by hand than by machine.

basic stitches

Use the following stitches to sew together the pattern pieces in this book.

Running Stitch: This essential stitch can be used for very simple hems, sewing two pieces of fabric together, and gathering fabric. To sew, simply draw the needle in and out of the fabric from right to left.

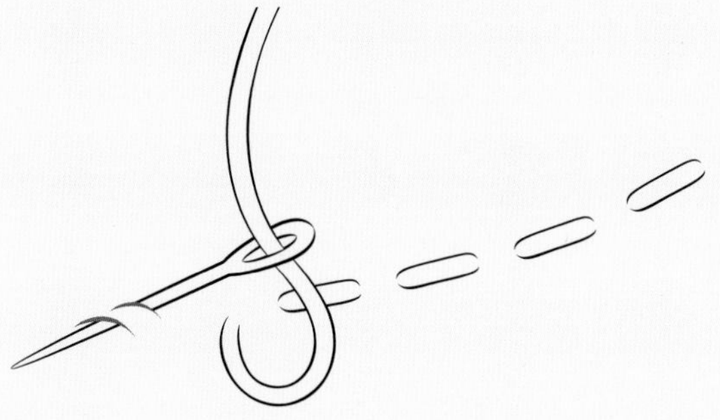

Back Stitch: This secure seam stitch is well suited to bulky seams and thicker fabric such as denim. Begin the stitch with a running stitch. Draw the needle out and back across the right side of the fabric, into the previous stitch.

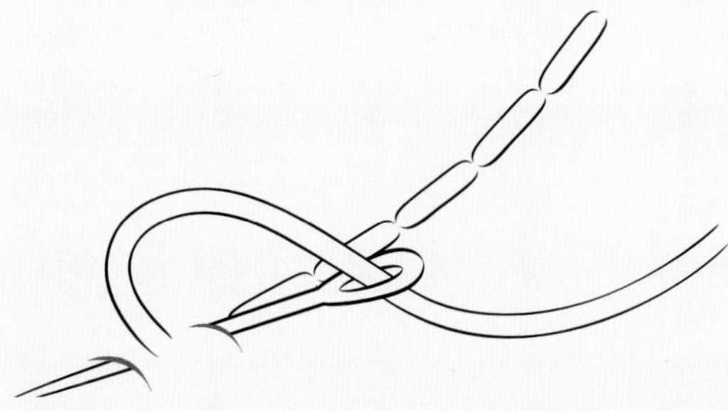

Blind Hem: As the name implies, this wonderful stitch creates a hem where you might not want the stitches to show on the right side, such as the hem of a pair of pants. Fold or layer fabric as desired. Draw the needle through the raw hem edge and pick up a tiny bit of the right-side fabric. Draw the needle in and loosely pull through the hem edge.

Decorative Stitches

Decorative embroidery stitches allow your creative spirit to fly and will impress your child with even the smallest detail. Sew up the simple white Ribbon Dress (page 149) and embroider sweet little stars along the bottom edge, or have your child draw a fun design on the dress with fabric chalk for you to stitch over in colors they choose. The Grayson Felted Crown (page 110) is the perfect project on which to practice your stitches.

Blanket Stitch: This stitch creates a decorative outline and is perfect for edging. Anchor the thread below the fabric edge. Draw the needle through the fabric to make a loop parallel to and the same width from the anchor. Bring the needle through the loop at the top edge.

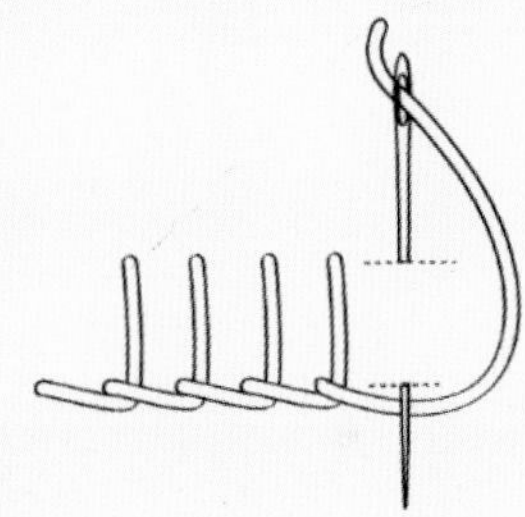

Satin Stitch: This stitch can be used to create solid circles that look like small round jewels. Draw the needle across the shape you wish to stitch, using a straight stitch.

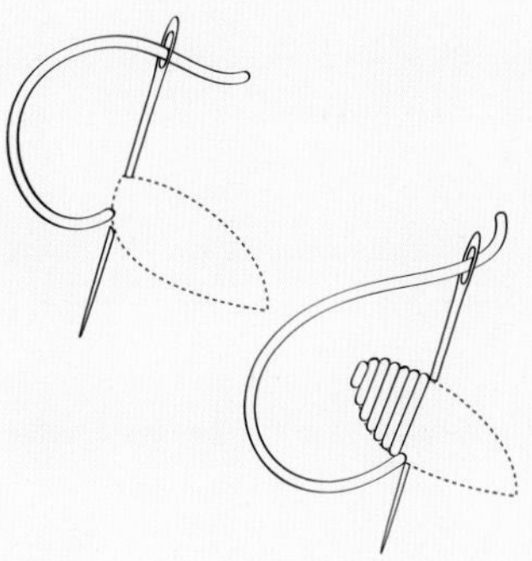

Split Stitch: This pretty stitch looks lovely as the stem of a flower or as a swirled outline. Using a multistrand embroidery floss or soft cotton thread, begin with a running stitch and then draw the needle back and through the previous stitch, splitting the strands.

tip: If winding a bobbin is all that stops you from using your sewing machine, pop into a craft or sewing store with a bobbin from your machine. There you can buy prespun bobbins in multiple colors—perfect for pragmatic seamstresses like me. There's no shame in shortcuts. For the first six months that I used my sewing machine, I had my husband thread the machine, and he doesn't even know how to sew!

PREPARATION IS KEY

Sewing doll clothing does not have to be an exact science. For some of the more complex patterns in this book, such as T-shirt and Jeans, I recommend that you prewash and press your fabric and pin down the seams before sewing. However, these simple patterns are designed for lazy seamstresses, like me, who just like to sit down and start sewing.

Most important is to have all your sewing supplies at hand, such as cotton thread, sewing needles, pins, fabric shears, a fabric marking pencil or tailor's chalk, an iron and ironing board, and measuring tape. Go ahead and make yourself a cute little sewing kit before you begin. It's like having a proper kitchen to cook in.

the jeans

Every child needs a pair of jeans to play in—and so does her doll. I like to use yellow (or other colored) thread to sew the leg hem and add faux details for a realistic jeans look.

materials

- Basic sewing supplies
- The Jeans Pattern (page 144)
- ½ yd (45.5cm) denim fabric, thin-to-medium weight
- 1 yd (0.9m) elastic, ½" (13mm) wide
- Safety pin

STEP 1: Enlarge the patterns at the percent indicated, and cut out the pattern.

STEP 2: Pin or trace the paper patterns onto the fabric, orienting the most stretchy direction of the fabric as indicated. Cut out 1 Waistband and 2 Back and 2 Front pieces.

STEP 3: With right sides facing, pin and sew together a Front and a Back piece along the outside leg seam only. Repeat for the second set of Front and Back pieces.

STEP 4: With right sides facing, line up CF Front to CF Back and CB Front to CB Back. Sew up the crotch seam and reorganize the fabric to create the legs.

STEP 5: Sew a simple ¼" (6mm) hem at the bottom of the legs, or skip this step to later fold under the cuffs to the desired length.

STEP 6: Press and sew the leg seams: Beginning at the bottom of one leg, sew up and then down the opposite leg seam in one large arch.

STEP 7: With right sides facing, fold the waistband piece in half widthwise and sew together the ends to make a closed loop.

STEP 8: Turn the jeans right side out and pin the Waistband to the top waist edge, right sides facing. Sew the Waistband to the pants using a ⅛" (3mm) seam allowance.

STEP 9: Turn the pants wrong side out. Fold and pin the Waistband over the raw edge about halfway to the sewn line to make the elastic casing. Sew around using a ⅛" (3mm) seam allowance, beginning at the center back and leaving a 1" (2.5cm) opening.

STEP 10: Cut a 10" (25.5cm) length of elastic. Attach the safety pin to one end of the elastic and push it through the casing. Sew the ends of the elastic together and close up the back opening.

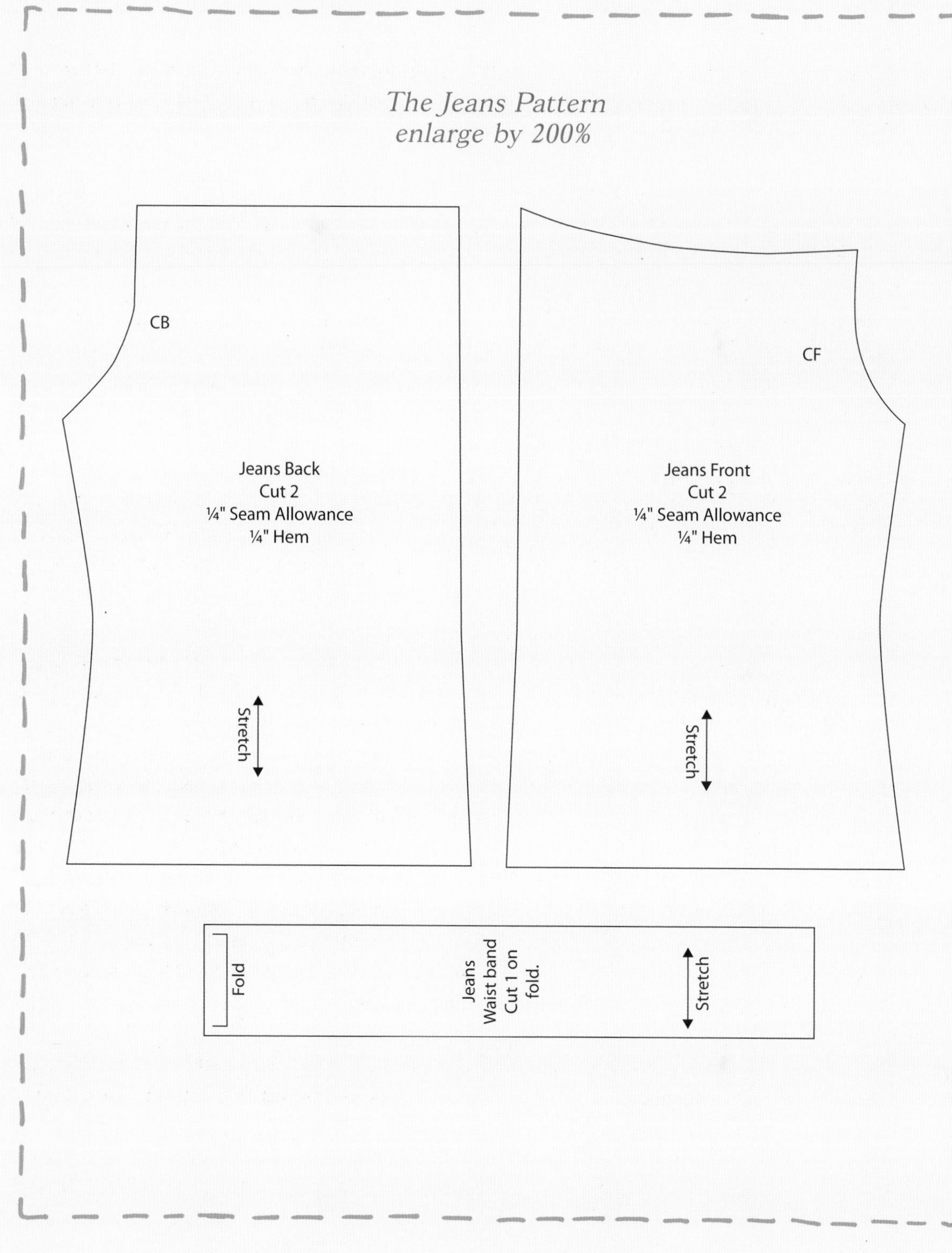
The Jeans Pattern
enlarge by 200%
CB
Jeans Back
Cut 2
¼" Seam Allowance
¼" Hem
Stretch
CF
Jeans Front
Cut 2
¼" Seam Allowance
¼" Hem
Stretch
Fold
Jeans
Waist band
Cut 1 on
fold.
Stretch

the t-shirt

My girls always wanted their dolls to wear T-shirts that matched their own, but a plain knit T-shirt with no brands, no words, and no embroidery was hard to find in the doll world. Now, with this basic pattern, I can sew doll-size T-shirts in any color they like.

materials

- Basic sewing supplies
- The T-Shirt Pattern (page 146)
- ½ yd (45.5cm) knit fabric
- 3 sew-on snaps or other fasteners

tip: When feeding knit fabric through your machine, pull gently only when necessary. Pulling will permanently stretch out the fabric as you sew. If you find yourself struggling, try using a ballpoint needle in the machine or a walking foot.

STEP 1: Enlarge the patterns at the percent indicated, and cut out the pattern.

STEP 2: Pin or trace the paper patterns onto the fabric, orienting the most stretchy direction of the fabric as indicated. Cut out 2 Back pieces, 1 Front piece, and 2 Sleeves. Copy the necessary markings from the patterns onto the fabric pieces.

STEP 3: With right sides together, sew each Sleeve to the Front using a ¼" (6mm) seam allowance. Then sew each Back piece to its corresponding Sleeve.

STEP 4: Press and sew each side seam: Beginning at the bottom edge, sew up and through the underarm and sleeve seams in one large arch.

STEP 5: Hem the sleeves using a ¼" (6mm) seam allowance and a zigzag stitch, if available. Then hem the bottom edge and the neckline.

STEP 6: Hand-sew the snaps or other closure onto the overlapping Back pieces as desired.

Note: Wool doll hair may catch and fray on hook-and-loop tape.

tip: Knit fabric does not fray the same way that a woven fabric will, so you can leave the edges raw if you like.

The T-Shirt Pattern
enlarge by 200%

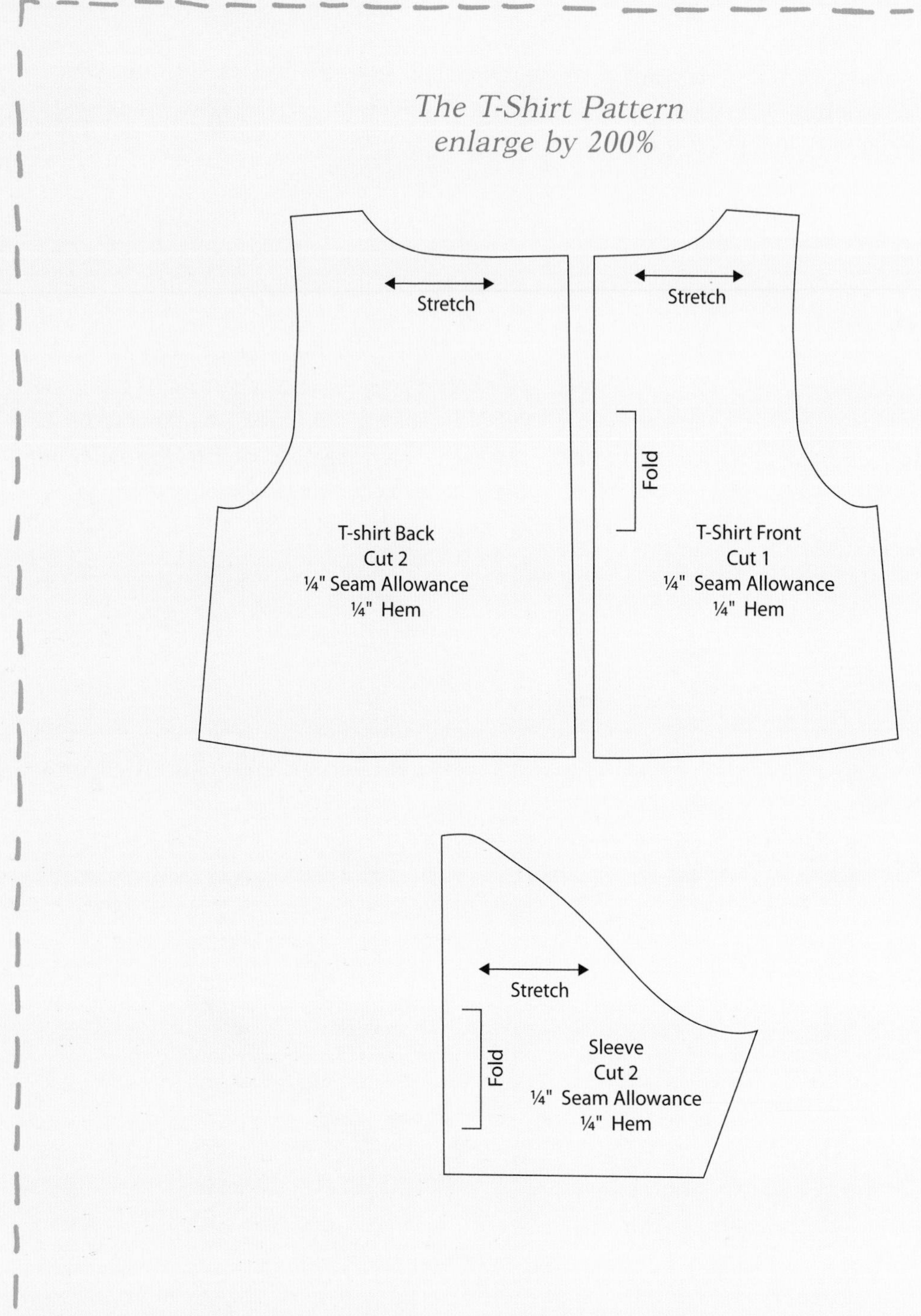

the leggings

Leggings layer perfectly under dresses and skirts and seem to have replaced tights in the modern girl's wardrobe. When choosing fabric for this pattern, check that it has good stretch in both directions, which allows you to forgo adding an elastic waistband.

materials

- Basic sewing supplies
- The Leggings Pattern (page 148)
- ½ yd (45.5cm) knit fabric, stretching in both directions

STEP 1: Enlarge the pattern at the percent indicated, and cut out the pattern.

STEP 2: Pin or trace the paper pattern onto the fabric, orienting the most stretchy direction of the fabric as indicated. Cut out two pattern pieces and mark one piece as the Front and the other as the Back. Copy the necessary markings onto the fabric pieces.

STEP 3: Line up CF Front to CF Back and CB Front to CB Back, right sides together. Sew up the crotch seam only. Pick up what you have just sewn and reorganize the fabric to create the legs.

STEP 4: Hem the legs and the waist using a ¼" (6mm) seam allowance.

STEP 5: Press and sew the leg seams: Beginning at the bottom of one leg, sew up and then down the opposite leg seam in one large arch.

tip: When feeding knit fabric through your machine, pull gently and only when necessary. Pulling will permanently stretch out the fabric as you sew. If you find yourself struggling, try using a ballpoint needle in the machine or a walking foot.

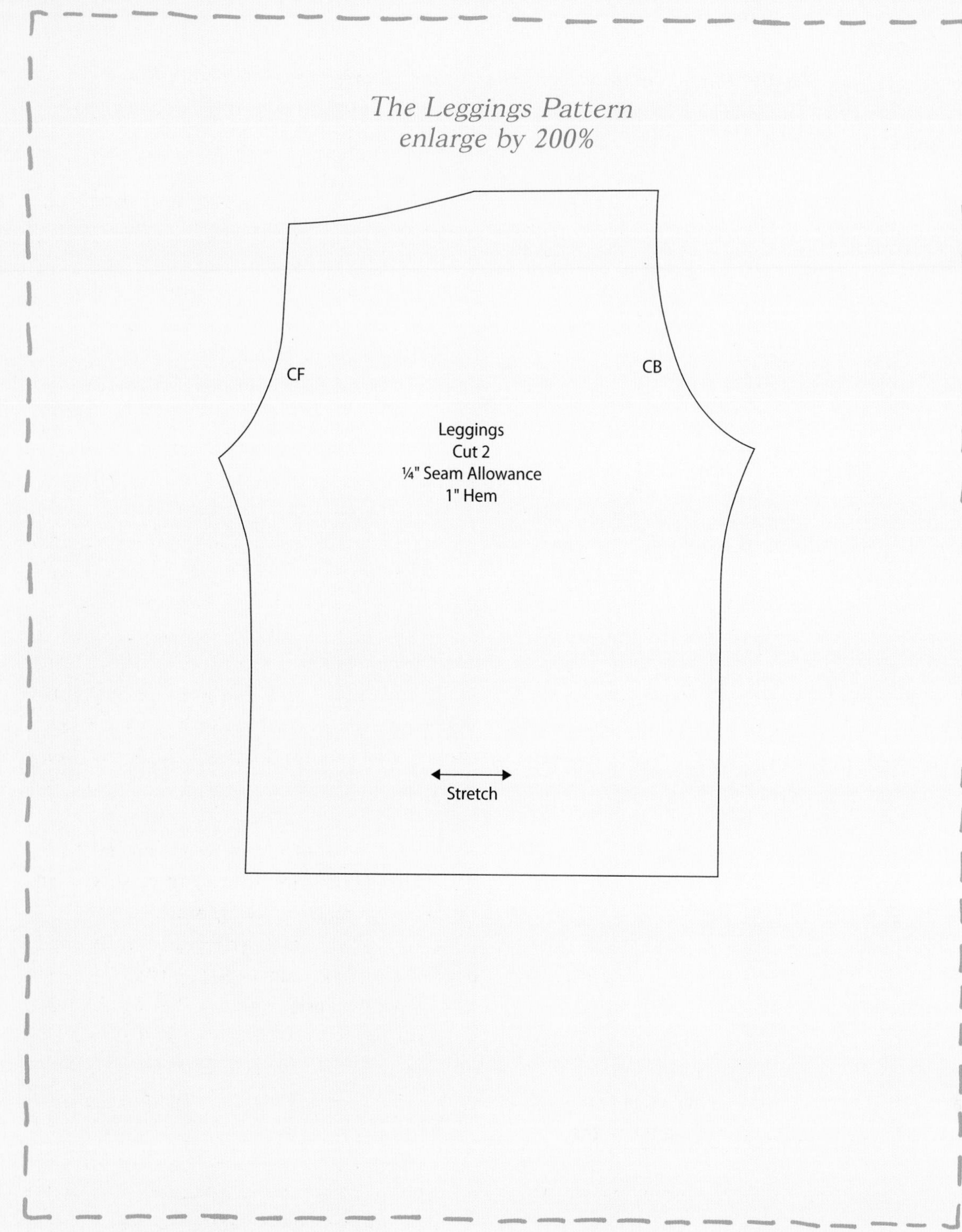
The Leggings Pattern
enlarge by 200%
CF
CB
Leggings
Cut 2
¼" Seam Allowance
1" Hem
Stretch

the ribbon dress

Leave it to my friend Jen to think of this clever ribbon-gathered dress pattern. Custom-fit the neckline for any toy—simply tie the ribbon loosely for portly teddies or more tightly for slender-necked dolls.

materials

- Basic sewing supplies
- 1 fat quarter of fabric (18 x 22" [45.5 x 56cm])
- 1 yd (.9m) ribbon, ½" (13mm) wide
- Safety pin

STEP 1: Fold the fabric in half lengthwise and cut along the fold.

STEP 2: Stack the fabric pieces with right sides facing. Mark the top with a pencil or chalk. Mark each side edge 4" (10cm) from the top of the fabric.

STEP 3: Beginning at the bottom edge, sew together the side edges using a ¼" (6mm) seam allowance, ending at each 4" (10cm) mark.

STEP 4: Press a ¼" (6mm) seam along each top, unsewn side edge—4 total underarm seams. Sew each seam individually, making sure not to sew together the back and front pieces of fabric.

STEP 5: Press a ½" (13mm) seam on the bottom hem and sew around.

STEP 6: Using your fingers or an iron, press the top front edge ¾" (2cm) to the wrong side and sew as close to the rough edge as possible to make the ribbon casing. Repeat for the top back edge.

STEP 7: Cut a 28" (71cm) length of ribbon. Attach the safety pin to one end of the ribbon and push the safety pin through both front and back ribbon casings.

STEP 8: Bunch the fabric onto the ribbon so that it forms a 4" (10cm) front and 4" (10cm) back, and create a left shoulder strap by exposing just 1" (2.5cm) of ribbon—all extra ribbon should be coming out at the right shoulder to be tied later. Pin down all 4 corners and use a locking stitch, or hand-sew a few stitches to keep the gathered material and ribbon and left shoulder in place. When you've dressed the doll, tie the ribbon to close.

tip: A fat quarter is sometimes a bit wide depending on your doll and fabric thickness, so you may choose to trim 2" (5cm) off one side before sewing.

the ruffle skirt

Sewing a unique-style skirt often means working with a complicated structure of many pattern pieces, but not when you jazz up a basic pattern with special fabric! A small stash of ruffle fabric and pretty elastic make this easy pattern stand out.

materials

- Basic sewing supplies
- ½ yd (45.5cm) ruffle fabric, see Resources (page 156)
- ½ yd (45.5cm) elastic, 1" (2.5cm) wide

STEP 1: Cut a rectangle from the fabric, 12½ x 5½" (32 x 14cm).

STEP 2: Cut a 12½" (32cm) length of elastic.

STEP 3: With the right side of the ruffle fabric facing you, fold the elastic over the entire top edge and pin it in place. Sew as close as possible to the bottom edge of the elastic, making sure to go through all three layers of fabric. Gently pull the fabric to feed it through the machine as you sew, but keep in mind that the more you pull, the more permanently stretched-out the fabric will become.

STEP 4: With right sides facing in, fold the fabric in half widthwise to create a tube and sew the two ends together using a ¼" (6mm) seam allowance. Turn the finished skirt right side out.

tip: This skirt can double as a halter top as shown with the Michelle Mermaid Tail (page 99). To make a dress, just add length.

Special Stitches and Techniques

The following techniques and stitches have been used in many of the patterns in this book. For more help with knitting techniques I highly recommend the many resources you'll find at your local yarn and book stores, which helped me when I was first learning to knit.

Backward-Loop Cast-on

This cast-on is incredibly easy—and useful for making increase stitches. Make a backward-facing loop with the working yarn and place it on the right-hand needle. Tighten as needed to maintain gauge. Repeat as needed.

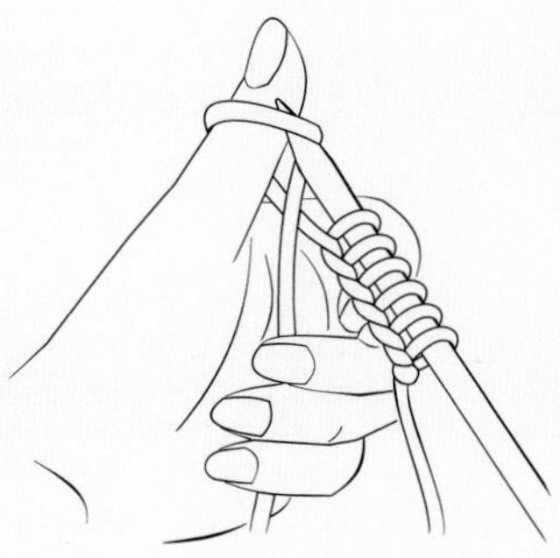

Baseball Stitch

This stitch is perfect for joining two seams without overlap, as for the Grayson Felted Crown (page 112). Each stitch should begin at the back of the work and come through to the front. Going between the two sides, insert an embroidery needle under the bottom left edge, bring it out ⅛ (3mm) from the edge, and pull it up through the fabric. Then insert the needle between the edges again and bring it out from the right edge this time, pulling the work together after each stitch. Repeat up the entire back opening. Work closely together for a secure seam.

Blocking

Wet blocking is an important part of the knitting process. Blocking will smooth out stitches and lace patterns, resulting in a cleaner and more finished-looking knit. You may be able to use blocking to correct small gauge issues or uneven stitches.

First, fill a sink or bathtub with warm water and add desired wool wash. Do not agitate or create bubbles. Then place the hand-knit item into the water, ensuring that object is fully submerged. Again, do not agitate. (This is important!) Leave the item to soak for about a half hour to an hour. Read a book, catch up on your e-mail, or pour yourself that cocktail. Now, remove the item from the water, cup it in your hands, and gently squeeze out any excess water. Lay it flat on a towel, and then roll up the towel and press it with your hands or knees so that the towel soaks up as much water as possible. Gently remove the item from the towel, and place it on a blocking board or other soft surface. Pin the item to the desired shape and dimensions, patting the fabric and smoothing it as needed. Always refer to the pattern size and schematic as a guide so you don't stretch out the fabric.

Cable Cast-on

For its use in this book, this cast-on is worked when there are already stitches present on the needle; at least 2 stitches must be on the needles in order to work this cast-on.

First, place the right-hand needle between the last two stitches on left-hand needle, wrap the working yarn, and bring the yarn through as if to knit. Transfer the newly created stitch onto the left-hand needle. Repeat this step as many times as necessary for the cast-on number.

Crochet Foundation Chain

The crochet foundation chain is simply a chain of slip stitches. Make a slipknot on the crochet hook. Then use the hook to grab the working end of the yarn and pull it through the slipknot, creating another stitch. Repeat to create the chain.

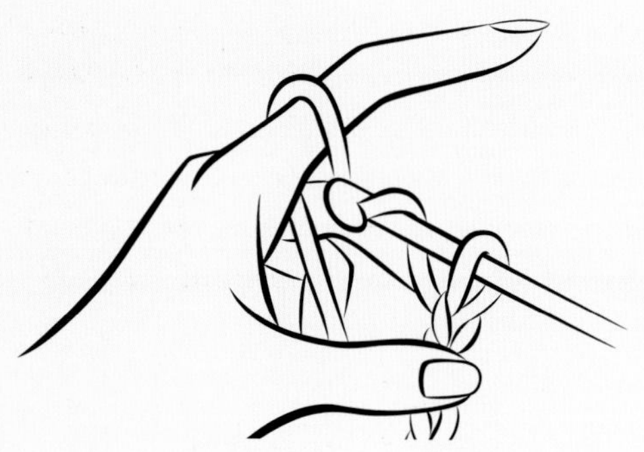

Crochet Slip Stitch

Crochet slip stitch is similar to the crochet foundation chain; you will pick up stitches from the knitting fabric instead of starting with a slipknot. Crochet slip stitch adds stability to any edge, but be sure to keep your tension even. If you find the last few stitches are too tight, simply pull out and rework.

STEP 1: Insert the crochet hook into the edge of the knitting at which you would like to begin and pull the working end of the yarn through. One loop is now on the crochet hook.

STEP 2: Insert the hook into the next stitch to be picked up and worked. There are now two loops on the crochet hook.

STEP 3: Wrap the working yarn around the hook tip and pull through *both* loops. You have now worked 1 slip stitch.

Repeat steps 2 and 3 until you reach the end of your edging.

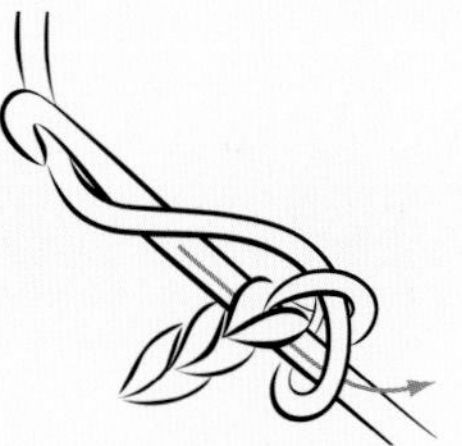

Single Crochet

The single crochet stitch, like the slipped stitch, makes a beautiful edging for knitwear. To work this stitch, follow the steps for slipped stitch crochet, with one notable difference in step 2.

STEP 1: Insert the crochet hook into the edge of the knitting and pull the working end of the yarn through. One loop is now on the crochet hook.

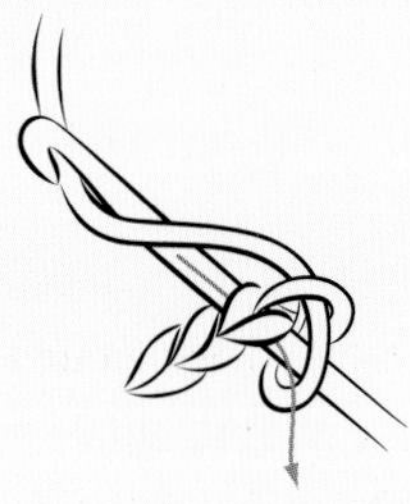

STEP 2: Insert the hook into the next stitch to be picked up and worked, *wrap the working yarn around the hook tip and pull through.* There are now two loops on the crochet hook.

STEP 3: Wrap the working yarn around the hook tip and pull through both loops. You now have worked 1 single crochet.

Repeat steps 2 and 3 until you reach the end of the edging.

Grafting

Grafting is used to seam two knit pieces together. Needles should be held parallel with both tips facing the same direction, and the wrong side of the fabric facing each other. Stitches are divided evenly across the two needles.

Setup: Insert a darning needle into the first stitch on the *front* needle as if to purl and pull through. Do not remove that stitch from the front needle. Then insert the darning needle into the first stitch on the *back* needle as if to knit and pull through. Do not remove the stitch from the front needle.

STEP 1: Insert the darning needle into first stitch on *front* needle as if to knit and slip the stitch off the end of the needle.

STEP 2: Insert the darning needle into the second stitch on *front* needle as if to purl, but do not remove the stitch from the needle. Gently pull the yarn to match the tension worked in the garment.

STEP 3: Insert the darning needle into the first stitch on the *back* needle as if to purl and slip the stitch off the end of the needle.

STEP 4: Insert the darning needle into the second stitch on the *back* needle as if to knit, but do not remove the stitch from the needle. Gently pull the yarn to match the tension worked in the garment.

Repeat steps 1–4 until all stitches have been worked and slipped off the needles, making sure to gently pull the yarn as you go.

K1, P1 Rib

This basic rib stitch is used for simple, clean borders and edges.

Round/Row 1: *Knit 1, purl 1 *repeat to end of round/row.

Round/Row 2: Knit the knit stitches and purl the purl stitches.

Magic Loop Method

The Magic Loop method allows you to knit a garment on one long circular needle, at least 32" or 40" (81 or 101.5cm) in length. The longer the needle, the better.

STEP 1: Cast on the required number of stitches onto a long circular needle. Divide the stitches evenly between the front and back tips of the needle.

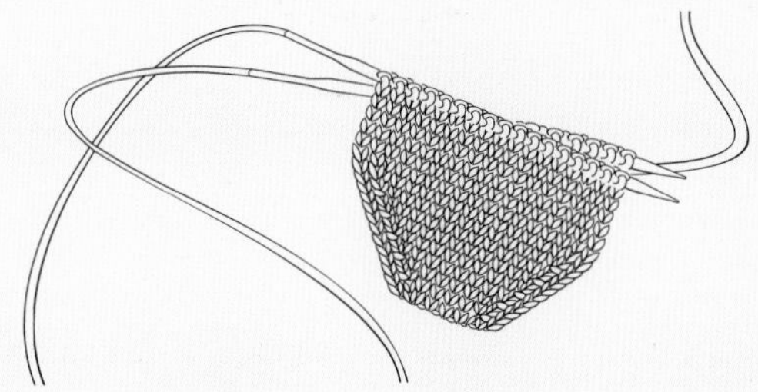

STEP 2: Slide the stitches from the back tip onto the cable, being careful not to allow them to get mixed up with the front stitches. You may now use the back needle to knit from the front needle and will have 2 loops of "open cable" to the left and right of your work.

STEP 3: Now comes the magic. Knit all front stitches onto the right-hand needle. At the end of this row, only half of the stitches in the round have been knit. Turn the work around and rearrange the stitches so that the unworked second half of the round is now in the front on the left needle, ready to be worked onto an empty right needle.

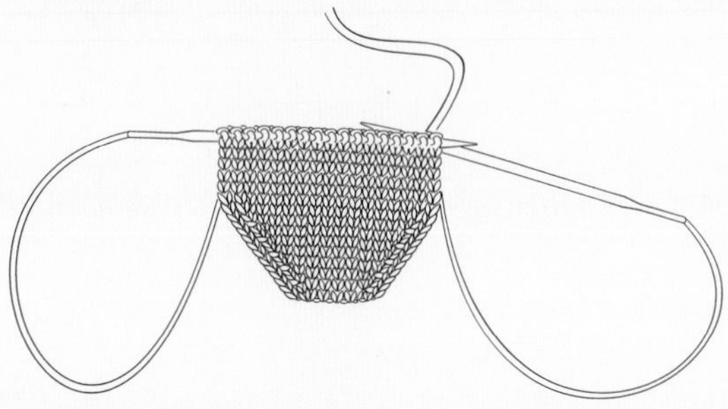

Repeat steps 2 and 3 to continue working in the round using the Magic Loop method. You may want to mark the beginning of the round with a safety pin or detachable stitch marker at the cast-on edge.

Three-Needle Bind-off

This bind-off is often used to close the toe on a sock or the top of a circular tube, but you can use it to bind off any item knit in the round that needs to be closed. For this particular technique you will need to have 3 needles total—hence the name.

STEP 1: Divide the stitches evenly onto two needles with the right sides of the fabric facing. Hold the needles in your left hand.

STEP 2: Holding the third needle your right hand, insert the needle as if to knit into the first stitch on both the front and back needles at the same time. Wrap the working yarn around the needle and "knit" the yarn through both stitches to make 1 new stitch on the right-hand needle. Repeat to knit a second stitch—2 stitches on the right-hand needle.

STEP 3: Lift the first stitch on the right-hand needle over the second stitch to bind off.

STEP 4: Continue to work steps 2 and 3 until all stitches have been bound off.

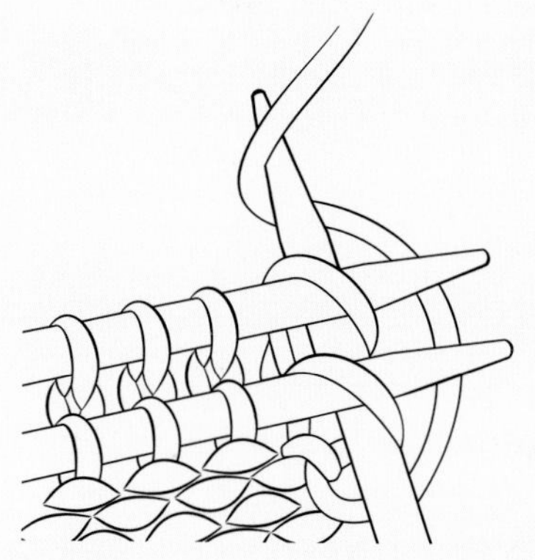

Abbreviations

CC – contrasting color
k – knit
k2tog – k2 together
kfb – knit into the front and back of a stitch
LC – left cross: Slip the indicated number of stitches (e.g., 2/2 LC) onto a cable needle and hold to the front of the work; knit the indicated number of stitches; knit the stitches from the cable needle
m1 – make 1: Lift the bar between the stitches and knit it through the back loop.
MC – main color
p – purl
p2tog – purl 2 together
pfb – purl into the front and back of a stitch
psso – pass slipped stitch over
RC – right cross: Slip the indicated number of stitches (e.g., 2/2 RC) onto a cable needle and hold to the back of the work; knit the indicated number of stitches; knit the stitches from the cable needle
RT – right twist: K2tog but do not drop stitches from the needle; knit the first stitch again through the 2 stitches; slip both stitches.
skp – slip, knit, psso: Slip 1 knitwise, k1, pass the slipped stitch over.
sk2p – slip, knit 2 together, psso: Slip 1 knitwise, k2tog, pass the slipped stitch over.
sl – slip
ssk – slip, slip knit: [Slip 1 knitwise] twice, insert the left-hand needle into the fronts of these 2 stitches from left to right, k2tog through the back loops.
yo – yarn over

Standard yarn weight system

categories of yarn, gauge ranges, and recommended needle size

Yarn Weight Symbol and Category Names	1 super fine	2 fine	3 light	4 medium	5 bulky
Types of Yarn in Category	Lace, Sock, Fingering, Baby	Sport, Baby	DK, Light Worsted	Worsted, Aran	Chunky, Craft, Rug
Average Knitted Gauge over 4" (10cm)	27–32 sts	23–26 sts	21–24 sts	16–20 sts	12–15 sts
Recommended Needle in U.S. Size Range	1–3	3–5	5–7	7–9	9–11
Recommended Needle in Metric Size Range	2.25–3.25mm	3.25–3.75mm	3.75–4.5mm	4.5–5.5mm	5.5–8mm

* GUIDELINES ONLY : The above chart reflects the most commonly used gauges and needle sizes for specific yarn categories.

** Lace weight yarns are usually knitted on larger needles to create lacy, openwork patterns. Accordingly, a gauge range is difficult to determine. Always follow the gauge stated in your pattern.

Skill Levels Explained

I designed the patterns in this book to be accessible for knitters at all skill levels. These designations can be used to help guide you when choosing a project.

Easy—If you are new to knitting, or are just looking for a quick, straightforward knit, start with an Easy project, which uses simple construction methods and avoids fancy stitches. These patterns feature purl and knit stitches and the occasional increase or decrease. *Technique examples:* Raglan shaping, seed stitch, and sleeve shaping.

Intermediate—These patterns feature slightly more complicated construction methods, repeating stitch patterns, decorative stitches, and chart reading. *Technique examples:* Knitting with beads, yarn overs, Fair Isle, and socks.

Advanced—The most involved patterns use techniques such as cables, complex construction and shaping, advanced stitch patterns, and large charts. *Technique examples:* Working two different patterns or repeats at the same time and cables.

Resources

The following resources include the yarns used in this book, wonderful shops for fabric and DIY doll-making materials, and reliable places to find unique and modern handcrafted doll clothing, as well as a few places to find adorable fashions for children—to style under all those hand-knits. All of the companies listed below are those that I have used in the past and can recommend.

Yarn

The knitting patterns in this book were made using yarn from the following companies:

Blue Sky Alpacas
888-460-8862
Blueskyalpacas.com

Cascade Yarns
Cascadeyarns.com

Debbie Bliss
Debbieblissonline.com

Elsebeth Lavold
516-546-3600
Knittingfever.com/c/elsebeth-lavold/yarn

Lorna's Laces
773-935-3803
Lornaslaces.net

Noro
516-546-3600
Knittingfever.com/c/noro/yarn

Red Heart
800-648-1479
Redheart.com

Spud & Chloë
888-460-8862
Spudandchloe.com

Sublime
516-546-3600
Knittingfever.com/c/sublime/yarn

SweetGeorgia Yarns
604-569-6811
Sweetgeorgiayarns.com

Fabric & Clothing

Many of the doll clothes featured in this book were sewn using Sarah Jane's timeless line of cotton fabrics, available through select retailers and online at sarahjanestudios.com. Other fabric designers popular for handmade doll and children's clothing include Amy Butler, Rashida Coleman-Hale, Alexander Henry, Anna Maria Horner, Michael Miller, and Heather Ross.

As with yarn, it's always best to choose fabric in person to gauge color, texture, and weight for yourself. Your local fabric or quilt shop likely carries a few of these popular brands, which also are available online.

Fabric

Fabric Worm

805-239-8888

For designer, organic, knit, and linen fabrics; Japanese imports

Fabricworm.com

Ruffle Fabric & Elastic

For ruffle fabric

Rufflefabric.com

LolaPink Fabric

For designer and organic fabrics and bundles

Etsy.com/shop/LolaPinkFabrics

Lucky Kaeru Fabric and Supplies

For Japanese imports, retro and bundled fabrics

Etsy.com/shop/luckykaerufabric

Clothing

The following shops are my favorites for online inspiration. I've personally purchased from them all—and many of the kids photographed in this book are wearing clothes made by these designers. When shopping for vintage and new kid and doll clothes online, I often search Etsy.com. Small mom-and-pop online shops may sell out quickly—even the same day—so be sure to check in often.

Lillipops Designs

For vintage-inspired, whimsical clothes with a fun attitude.

Designer Jayme Lillie has an eye for classic color with a modern twist.

Lillipopsdesigns.com

The Measure

For seasonal collections with a modern-vintage point of view.

Themeasuredesigns.com

The Melamoose Co.

For funky fabric combinations, ruffles, gathers, and layers galore.

Can be found on Etsy.com and Facebook.com under the name TheMelamooseCo.

Molly's Playground

For doll coats and jackets

Can be found on Etsy.com and Facebook.com under the name MollysPlayground.

Reggiesdolls

For costumes and shoes

Can be found on Etsy.com and Facebook.com under the name ReggiesDolls.

ZozoBugBaby

For matching patchwork doll and kid-size bedding.

Julie Martin designs clothing full of spunk and color with a vintage and bohemian feel.

Zozobugbaby.com

Meet the Dolls

The doll makers listed below represent those whom I have firsthand experience with—my children have seen and played with dolls from each of these talented doll makers. Representing several different countries, they are among the most accessible and readily available artists.

Well-made and handcrafted goods can sometimes be a bit expensive. One very happy alternative is to make one. A handmade doll is an incredible treasure, twice over when the recipient knows that you made it yourself, just for them. To find out more, visit Weirdollsandcrafts.com, www.joyswaldorfdolls.com, and Pollika.com, or check out the book *Making Waldorf Dolls* by Maricristin Sealey (Hawthorn Press, 2005).

Custom-made to look like my older daughter, Sydney's doll (page 5) is one of my favorites from the Canadian company **Bamboletta**, which makes dolls using only natural materials. A group of "sewing mommas" makes each Bamboletta doll by hand, under the direction of owner Christina Platt. Platt hand-dyes the yarn used for the dolls' hair, and she often mixes together several dye lots to give the dolls a natural and funky look. She puts up a collection of dolls for sale every Friday night—and they sell out faster than you can say "Bamboletta."

Bamboletta.com

Katie (page 7) is a **Fig and Me** doll, created by Fabiola Pérez-Sitko. She believes that children grow best when surrounded by natural energy and materials, and her dolls have a particular whimsy to their sweet chubby faces, sure to spur young imaginations. Each doll comes dressed in unique hand-sewn and hand-knit clothing—and her doll backpacks are to die for.

Figandme.com

Other popular handmade cloth dolls come from the following makers:

Aunt Boo's Babies creates adorable dolls, many of which are sweet newborns with precious faces. Barbara's ("Aunt Boo") dark-haired, olive-skinned dolls remind me of my diverse family and are among my favorites.

Etsy.com under the name AuntBoosBabies

Dragonfly's Hollow's dolls, full of magic, were originally inspired by Margery Williams's story *The*

Velveteen Rabbit, and maker Nancy McLaughlin's six children.
Dragonflyshollow.com

Fabrique Romantique is based in the Netherlands and makes each doll with delicate detailing. For me, these dolls hold earthy and timeless qualities.
Fabriqueromantique.com

Little Jenny Wren Dolls are custom made by Jenny Marshall in a multitude of sizes, prices, and hairstyles, with particularly cute 12" (30.5cm) dolls.
Littlejennywren.blogspot.com

Tumbleberry Toys dolls come in eight different styles. Many are traditionally sewn, but doll maker Jen Davenport also offers snuggle dolls and baby dolls with jointed limbs.
Tumbleberrytoys.com

Acknowledgments

It would be impossible to mention all the numerous people who, if even in a small way, have had a part in this book—from the friends who originally pushed me to write patterns on my own to the many gals of the North Georgia Knitters and the Friday Night Atlanta SIP crew, who never cease to continue cheering me on and providing moral support.

Below are a few of the people who have helped me create the book you now hold in your hands. It does, without a doubt, take a village.

Susan B. Anderson, unfailingly supportive and encouraging,

Joan Bebe and Eve Ng, two amazing technical editors,

Linsay Cocker and Jaclyn Jaquette, cheery and fast test knitters,

Jennifer and Jared Fleury of Fleury Sheep & Wool, who allowed me to use their farm and many other wonderful things,

Kate Atherley, Laura Chau, Marnie MacLean and Brett Parker, Linda Roghaar, Cathy Scott of StitchMastery, Allegra Wermuth, and Primrose Childcare—and Betty Wong and Rebecca Behan, who never gave up on me.

Many thanks go to my mother and father, who never stopped telling me I could do anything I put my mind to, to my husband for taking on the kids without question during that last week of writing, to my mother-in-law, Marge, for always asking me how the book was coming along, and to Claudia Purgason, the most prolific knitter I know and the best friend a girl can have.

And finally, I must thank my big sister, who played dolls with me when we were small, and the doll makers who hand-stitched each doll in this book. It would not have been possible without them, as they inspired this work from the start.

Index